Good to Eat

ALSO BY BURT WOLF

Gatherings and Celebrations

Burt Wolf's Menu Cookbook

Burt Wolf's Table

Eating Well

BURT WOLF

Good to Eat

Flavorful Recipes from
One of Television's Best-Known
Food and Travel Journalists

DOUBLEDAY

NEW YORK | LONDON | TORONTO
SYDNEY | AUCKLAND

PUBLISHED BY DOUBLEDAY
a division of Random House, Inc.
1540 Broadway, New York, New York 10036

DOUBLEDAY and the portrayal of an anchor with a dolphin are
trademarks of Doubleday, a division of Random House, Inc.

Book design by Christopher Kuntze Design

Library of Congress Cataloging-in-Publication Data
Wolf, Burton.
    Good to eat: flavorful recipes from one of television's
best-known food and travel journalists / Burt Wolf. —1st ed.
        p.   cm.
    Includes index.
    1. Cookery, International.   I. Title.
TX725.A1W58313   1999
641.5—dc21   98-40695
                                                       CIP

ISBN 0-385-48266-3
Copyright © 1999 by Burt Wolf
All Rights Reserved
Printed in the United States of America
May 1999
First Edition
10 9 8 7 6 5 4 3 2 1

This book is dedicated to my grandson Max, who arrived at our table on August 8, 1998.

I hope he will always be able to find something good to eat.

ACKNOWLEDGMENTS

Emily Aronson was the Executive Producer for the television shows on which this book is based. *Caroline McCool* was the Senior Television Producer. *David Dean* was the Executive Editor of the series. *Michele Urvater* adapted the recipes that we taped on location and created the additional recipes to round out the book. It is as much her book as mine. *Mindy Hermann* guided me through the research on the relationship between food and good health. *Lise Bellefeuille* was the Associate Editor on both the book and the television series. *Raymond W. Merritt* of Willkie, Farr and Gallagher completed his twenth-ninth year as our legal advisor and most uncompromising critic. *Mort Janklow* and *Cullen Stanley* are our literary agents. *Ted Turner* at Cable News Network put me to work for CNN when it first went on the air, which made all of this possible. *Kevin Senie, Dalton Delan,* and *Pattie Newi* at The Travel Channel encouraged and funded much of my world travel. *Gene Nichols* at American Program Service in Boston and *Mike La Bonia* and his staff at WKNO in Memphis have been bringing my series to public television since 1992.

I would also like to thank the individual public television stations across the country that have accepted my series and featured them prominently in their schedules. This partnership has granted me the opportunity to share my love of good food, travel, and cultural history with viewers throughout the United States.

AND:

Ron V. Brown	Christopher Kuntze	Steven J. Ross
John Fulvio	Calliope Lappas	Bruce Stark
Kenneth Jackier	Anita Michael	Susan Van Velson
Judith Kern	Larry Ossias	Marjorie Wolff
Joel Kleiman	Janet Pappas	
Kip Knight	John Peaslee	

I AM NOT A DOCTOR

I am not a doctor, I don't even play one on television. I am a journalist interested in food, travel, and social history. Part of my work puts me in touch with scientists researching the relationship between what we eat and drink, and our health. The sections in this book that deal with medical and nutritional advice come from those contacts. They represent my reaction to these interviews and they are my personal beliefs at this moment (summer, 1998). I am sure that the science and my own ideas will change. Please do not take this information as medical advice, that can only come from your doctor.

Having made the above disclaimer, I should like to point out the following: Each year the percentage of the U.S. population over age fifty becomes greater and more of us confront health problems related to aging. Many of these difficulties can be avoided, and many can be corrected. The key to avoidance is a lifestyle that incorporates preventative measures that are well-known and scientifically accepted. Early detection through regular medical examination is essential.

The new world of managed health care is rationing many of the affordable options. Your own preventative measures are becoming more and more important, and it's never too early to start.

CONTENTS

Good to Eat

INTRODUCTION

The ancient Greeks had a saying, "The objective is to die as young as possible, as late in life as you can." I agree, and for the past thirty years I have been studying the research relating good food to good health and longevity. During those decades, it has become increasingly clear that what you eat can help protect against chronic diseases—obesity, heart disease, cancer, arthritis, and diabetes.

On the other hand, I am fully aware that the clock of ages keeps ticking, and though I may be able to slow it down and in some cases wind it back a little, eventually my present life will run out. The challenge is to find a balance between living a healthy life and wanting to have a good time.

From a gastronomic viewpoint, it is essential to remember that for the average person (without special health problems) there are no foods that will save your life and there are no foods that will kill you. It's all about appropriate quantities. This book is a chapter from the journal of my search for balance.

The first section of the book, "You Are What You Eat," will bring you up to date with what I believe to be the most reliable research and information on food and its effect on health and longevity. The remainder of the book contains the recipes and interesting facts that I collected during my travels.

I chose the title *Good to Eat* because it gave me a double-edged tool. Some of the recipes are in the book because they taste good and are "nutritionally" good for you. Other recipes have been included under the *Burt Wolf Scientifically As Yet Unproven Rules of Existence: Section II,* which states: "When something feels wonderful, the brain sends a signal to the entire body that it's 'good to be alive.'" This message is important to your health and should be pursued (within reason) as part of a regular program. It is the best way to keep up your appetite for life.

BURT WOLF
New York, New York
August 1998

YOU ARE WHAT YOU EAT

THREE MAJOR POINTS:

1. What you eat has a dramatic effect on your health.
2. It's never too late to improve your diet.
3. The older you get the more important it is to pay attention to what you eat.

CALORIES

A calorie is a measure of the energy in a food. One calorie is the amount of heat needed to raise the temperature of one liter of water by one degree. Scientists burn a specific food in a laboratory, measure the heat given off, and estimate the food's caloric value.

A gram of protein contains 4 calories.

A gram of carbohydrates contains 4 calories.

A gram of alcohol contains 7 calories.

A gram of fat contains 9 calories.

CARBOHYDRATES

The starches and sugars found in plants are called "carbohydrates" and they are divided into two types: The sugars are classified as simple carbohydrates and the starches are known as complex carbohydrates. Complex carbohydrates are considered better for you because they contain vitamins, minerals, and fiber.

PROTEIN

Muscle, skin, cartilage, and bone are made of protein. Protein contains the body's primary building blocks called "amino acids." Amino acids come in twenty-two different varieties and are essential for good health. Your body can produce thirteen amino acids, the other nine must come from foods.

THE FATS OF LIFE

A simple way to look at the subject of fat is to think of your body as a furnace or engine and the food you take in as its fuel. The energy that is produced when your body burns the food or fuel you eat is measured in calories. An ounce of fat contains about 250 calories.

When we talk about fat, the first distinction to make is between the body fat that is part of our physical structure and the dietary fat that we eat.

Body fat does some good things. About half of our body fat is stored just underneath our skin and because fat is a bad conductor of heat, it insulates us against extremes of both heat and cold. Fat is also a protective cushion for organs like the heart and kidneys. It is the storage container for our fuel. If we take in more fuel than we burn, our systems will convert the extra calories to body fat and store them in some annoying place like our hips or stomach. I would prefer an arrangement that took the first ten pounds of excess body fat and stored them on the bottom of my feet so I ended up taller, but nothing's perfect. If we burn more calories than we take in, our system turns our body fat back into fuel, burns it, and feeds us energy.

Like body fat, the fat we eat is also essential to good health. It helps us absorb vitamins A, D, E, and K and move them to the parts of our bodies where they are needed. Dietary fat is the magic carpet on which flavor travels. "No fat" can mean "no flavor." And for many foods, fat improves both texture and aroma. Because fats take longer to digest than proteins or carbohydrates, they spend more time in the stomach and give some people a greater sense of being full. I often find that taking many of my daily fat calories at breakfast reduces my hunger throughout the day.

The average person needs less than a tablespoon of dietary fat per day (about 11 grams), but most Americans take in six to eight tablespoons each day. And that's where the problems start. Excess dietary fat leads to excess body fat, which is associated with an increased risk of heart disease, cancer, and diabetes. Sometimes, too much of a good thing can kill you, and fat is a perfect example. The American Heart Association and the American Cancer Society both recommend a diet with no more than 30 percent of daily calories coming from fat, which for most people would be just under five tablespoons (65 grams).

Calories from fat are more easily stored in your body than calories from protein or carbohydrates. About a fourth of the calories in a carbohydrate food is burned up in the process of storing it. Only 3 percent of the calories in dietary fat are burned on the way to being stored as body fat. It is easier to get fat from eating fat than it is from eating carbohydrates or protein.

The Three Forms of Dietary Fat

In trying to understand fats, it is helpful to think of fat as a chain made up of links, like the links in a charm bracelet. Hanging from some links, like the little charms on the bracelet, are pairs of hydrogen atoms. If a pair of hydrogen atoms is hanging from every spot that could hold a pair, then the fat is said to be saturated, that is, saturated with hydrogen. It can also be called a "hydrogenated fat."

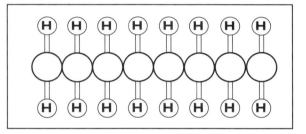

If there is room left for one pair of hydrogen atoms, the fat is said to be monounsaturated. If the fat chain can take on two or more pairs of hydrogen atoms, the fat is called "polyunsaturated." Unfortunately, there is nothing charming about these hydrogen atoms. Hydrogenated and saturated fats appear to be directly related to an increase in blood cholesterol levels and heart disease. Hydrogenated fats also contain *trans fatty acids* that increase blood cholesterol levels in much the same way as saturated fat. Recent research tags trans fatty acids as dangerous to our health.

Most of the fats and oils in our diet contain varying amounts of all three of these fats: saturated, monounsaturated, and polyunsaturated. However, we end up describing a fat or oil as saturated, monounsaturated, or polyunsaturated based on its having more of one form of fat than the other two.

About two thirds of the fat in dairy products is saturated, about half the fat in the fat that comes from beef and other hooved animals is saturated. Chicken and other poultry fat run a little lower in saturated fat. The fats and oils in fish are usually low in saturated fat, otherwise the oil would turn hard in cold water and make it impossible for the fish to swim. The more saturated or hydrogenated a fat is, the harder it will be both to your touch and your heart.

Most foods that come from animals (meats and dairy products) have higher levels of saturated fats than fruits and vegetables. Fruits and vegetables tend to have very little fat and the fat that they do have is usually monounsaturated and polyunsaturated. Exceptions are the *tropical oils:* coconut oil, palm kernel oil, palm oil, and cocoa butter, which are highly saturated.

The intake of saturated fat increases the level of cholesterol in our blood. Polyunsaturated and monounsaturated fats reduce cholesterol levels when they replace saturated fats in our diets.

In the language of fats, a fat that is a solid at room temperature is called a "fat." A fat that is liquid at room temperature is called an "oil." I use canola oil, which is a type of rapeseed oil. The word *canola* is a contraction of Canada and oil, a patriotic gesture by the Canadian scientists who developed it. Canola oil is very low in saturated fat and high in monounsaturated fat. It contains a number of fatty acids that have become associated with the reduction of heart disease. I also use olive oil, which is high in monounsaturates and polyunsaturates.

Hydrogenation

Sometimes manufacturers will take a polyunsaturated fat and saturate it with hydrogen atoms. They do this because polyunsaturated fat turns rancid faster than hydrogenated fat. Hydrogenated fats will also keep crackers and cookies crisp. Hydrogenation may preserve the fat and the manufacturers' profits, but it does nothing to preserve our good health.

Omega 3

The polyunsaturated fat in seafood contains a fatty acid known as Omega 3, which has gotten a great deal of publicity as a substance that may reduce the risk of heart disease. Scientists believe that Omega 3 may prevent the formation of clots that block the flow of blood to the heart. It may also reduce the pain of arthritis by reducing inflammation. As little as two servings of fish per week seem to have an effect. Fish from cold water contain the largest amounts of Omega 3:

herring, salmon, trout, sardines, and bluefin tuna. Fish oil supplements, however, are not the answer. They can be made from fish livers, which often contain toxic chemicals. The effectiveness of fish oil supplements is unproven and many respected authorities consider them unsafe.

CUTTING DOWN ON FATS

1. Choose lean cuts of meat, like loin, and remove the visible fat before cooking.

2. Remove poultry fat before cooking poultry. That helps avoid temptation and allows seasonings to go directly to the meat.

3. Avoid turkey and other poultry that has been prebasted by the injection of fat.

4. Most foods in a liquid state (soups and stews) can be chilled, which causes the fat to solidify and rise to the surface where it can be skimmed off. I keep my cans of chicken stock in the refrigerator and skim off the solidified fat before I use the stock.

5. Choose a cooking method that will allow the natural fat in the food to drip away: roasting on a rack, broiling, grilling.

6. Use non-stick cookware and coat it with as little oil as possible.

7. In most cases, I choose the low-fat form of the food: skimmed milk and milk products, low-fat mayonnaise and low-fat salad dressings. My love of ice cream, however, will accept no substitutions, though it will accept smaller portions than in the past.

8. Fish and shellfish contain less fat than meat and poultry, and the fat fish does contain tends to be polyunsaturated.

9. Try and keep the uncooked portion size of meat, fish, and poultry to 4 ounces, about the size of a deck of cards. If that proves too difficult, even things out with a vegetarian day.

EQUIPMENT THAT WILL HELP FAT-PROOF YOUR KITCHEN

1. *A ribbed frying pan with a non-stick surface* will allow you to cook meat, fish, and poultry without using additional cooking fat. It will also let some of the fat contained in the food drip away into the ribbing.

2. *A fat separator cup* has a pouring spout that draws liquids from the bottom of the cup. Since fat floats on the top, this device lets you separate gravy and stock and other liquids from much of their fat.

3. *A slotted broiler pan or broiler rack* that will allow fat to drip away from meat, fish, or poultry.

4. *A vertical roasting rack* that holds poultry in a position that will allow much of its fat to drip into a holding pan.

5. *An oil sprayer* that allows you to fill it with your own choice of oil. It can deliver a fine mist of oil on the cooking surfaces of your pots, pans, and grill racks or onto your ingredients, e.g., a salad. It can drastically reduce the amount of oil you use without reducing flavor.

CHOLESTEROL

We're talking plumbing. A subject that is terrifying for home owners and pretty serious for people interested in good health.

Blood travels through our bodies in a series of pipes called "blood vessels." One of the substances in our blood is cholesterol. It's similar to fat and we use it to strengthen cell membranes, produce vitamin D, form the coatings that protect nerves, and help digest fats. And that is just a partial list of the good things about cholesterol. Our bodies produce cholesterol in the liver. We make about 1,000 milligrams of cholesterol daily, and that's all the cholesterol we really need. Most Americans, however, take in additional cholesterol each day as part of their diet, which can raise the level of cholesterol in the blood. More important, the saturated fat in our diet, through some process we don't fully understand, raises the level of cholesterol in the blood even more than the cholesterol we eat. And here we are again—too much of a good thing becoming a killer.

When the level of cholesterol in the blood gets too high, it causes deposits of fat in the arteries and blood vessels. The deposits make it hard for blood to pass through the system. The condition is known as atherosclerosis and it is the leading cause of heart attacks in the United States.

Blood vessel with deposits of fat

The Good Guys and the Bad Guys

There are two major types of cholesterol: HDL and LDL. HDL appears to be good for us; it moves through our pipes and cleans out some of the deposits that are caused by LDL, the bad form of cholesterol. I remember which is which by thinking that the *H* in HDL stands for "heavenly" and the *L* in LDL stands for "lousy."

What Influences Cholesterol Levels

1. How your body deals with cholesterol is, to a certain extent, the result of your *genes*. Some folks have inherited genes that do a good job with cholesterol and some of us have yet another reason to complain about our parents. If that's your thing.
2. Being *overweight* increases blood cholesterol levels and at the same time reduces the good form of cholesterol. You end up with more of everything you don't want. Losing weight often reduces blood cholesterol levels.
3. Blood cholesterol levels tend to go up with *age*. Men under fifty usually have more of the bad cholesterol than women of the same age. After fifty, women get more of the bad stuff. That may be why women under fifty have fewer heart attacks than men, but tend to catch up later in life.
4. A diet high in *saturated fats* increases blood cholesterol levels. Saturated fat in your diet does more to increase blood cholesterol level than eating foods rich in cholesterol.

General Tips on Lowering Blood Cholesterol Levels
(After You Have Talked to Your Doctor)

1. Lose excess weight.
2. Eat a diet that is generally low in fat, and make a special effort to keep your diet low in saturated fats and cholesterol.
3. Avoid the tropical oils: coconut oil, palm oil, and palm kernel oil, which are highly saturated.
4. Set up a program of regular exercise. A simple half-hour walk, covering just a mile and a half, three times a week, can help. Exercise increases the level of good cholesterol and helps control weight.

5. Have two meals a week that include fish like salmon, halibut, tuna, lake trout, or swordfish.
6. Include foods that are high in fiber: oats, dried beans, lentils, and other legumes. These foods are high in a type of fiber that reduces levels of blood cholesterol.
7. Increase your intake of fruits and vegetables. Fruits and vegetables do not contain cholesterol.

I suspect that my plumber and my cardiologist are conspiring. My plumber has started explaining his work with the same words as my doctor, and my doctor is sending me bills that are almost as high as my plumber's.

The recommendation to keep your overall intake of calories from fat below 30 percent of your total calories is a general goal and not to be used on a food-by-food basis. I see people in markets reading the nutritional labeling on a package and rejecting the product because more than 30 percent of its calories come from fat. That misses the point. The objective is keeping the calories from fat below 30 percent of your total calories from all foods during a two- or three-day period. A piece of sirloin steak (trimmed of visible fat) may get 40 percent of its calories from fat, but if the remainder of the meal consists of a baked potato with low-fat dressing and steamed vegetables with balsamic vinegar, the overall calories from fat will come down to less than 20 percent. And if you want to spend a meal indulging yourself with a few high-fat foods, just make sure you even things out during the next few days.

One note of caution on high-fat meals: Research suggests that as we get older, our bodies have a reduced ability to process the fat in a large meal. A single high-fat meal tends to put more fat on our bodies than the same amount of fat taken over three smaller meals, and high-fat meals can have an immediate negative effect on your cardiovascular system. Moderation is always the best bet.

VITAMIN B_6, VITAMIN B_{12}, AND FOLIC ACID

Low levels of B_6, B_{12}, and folic acid in the diet and bloodstream have been linked to an increased risk of cancer, stroke, and heart disease. Low folic acid levels are also associated with birth defects, depression, and impaired response to antidepressant medication.

Good sources of folic acid are enriched breads and cereals, whole grains, oranges, orange juice, beans, and green vegetables. B_6 and B_{12} are found in lean meat, poultry, seafood, and low-fat dairy products.

FIBER

Fiber is a nondigestible part of plants. It comes in two forms: soluble (dissolves in water to form a gel), and insoluble, which does not dissolve in water. Soluble fiber is found in beans, oats, barley, and fruit. Insoluble fiber is contained in whole grains and vegetables. A diet high in vegetable fiber protects against colon cancer. Soluble fiber also tends to reduce blood cholesterol levels and the risk of heart attack. Two studies indicate that fiber from cereal can help prevent type 2 diabetes (the common form that often arrives as a result of aging and obesity). A diet high in insoluble fiber has also shown to protect against colon cancer.

CALCIUM AND VITAMIN D

Calcium passes through our bloodstream and is stored in our bones. It is an essential element for strong bones but it also affects blood pressure, blood clotting, and a dozen other important body functions. When your body needs more calcium than it's getting, it takes the calcium from your bones. Eventually, it can lead to osteoporosis. One out of every two women and one out of every four men will suffer a fracture as a result of osteoporosis.

Both men and women under fifty should have a daily calcium intake of 1,000 mg. Over age fifty, the intake for both should be 1,200 mg per day. Skim and low-fat dairy products are the best source of calcium, but you can also use calcium-fortified orange juice, broccoli, canned salmon with the bones in, and dark green leafy vegetables. Calcium supplements can be useful, but remember that the calcium called for by nutrition experts is called "elemental calcium." Commercial calcium supplements are made up of elemental calcium combined with an acid; calcium carbonate, and calcium citrate are common examples. Only 40 percent of calcium carbonate is the "elemental calcium" you need, so a 1,000 mg pill will only give you 400 mg of "elemental calcium." Calcium citrate contains 24 percent "elemental calcium." Keep an eye out for this when you are calculating your daily intake of calcium.

It's also essential to keep in mind that vitamin D helps your body absorb calcium and is a necessary part of an anti-osteoporosis diet. If you are taking calcium tablets, take them with meals and not close to bedtime. Calcium dissolves best when acid is in your stomach. The experts recommend a daily intake of 200 IU of calcium up to age fifty; 400 IU from ages fifty-one through seventy; and 600 IU after age seventy.

Exposure to sunlight will cause your body to produce vitamin D, but sun screen with a rating of SPF 8 or higher blocks the effect. During the winter months, the northern third of the United States does not get sufficient ultraviolet B light to generate the response. Low-fat dairy products, especially those fortified with vitamin D, and vitamin supplements are the answer.

POTASSIUM AND SODIUM

Two minerals, potassium and sodium, team up to control the balance of the fluid in your body. Sodium works outside the cells, potassium is on the inside; together they affect blood pressure. Studies have reported that a reduction in sodium intake and increases in potassium can lower blood pressure levels. It's also important to know that our blood pressure becomes more sensitive to sodium as we get older.

High levels of sodium can leech calcium from your bones. Research indicates that on an annual basis, every 2,000 mg of excess sodium will result in a 1 percent loss of bone structure. Daily sodium intake should be 2,400 mg, or lower. If you are concerned about your blood pressure, your doctor will set a lower limit.

At the same time that you are keeping the sodium level in your diet down, you should be keeping the potassium level up. The recommended amount is 2,000 mg per day. Good sources are bananas, oranges, orange juice, cantaloupe, potatoes, lentils, and beans.

FREE RADICALS AND ANTIOXIDANTS

As part of its natural metabolism, your body produces molecules known as free radicals. And like most radicals, they have both positive and negative aspects. Free radicals can fight dangerous bacteria; they can also contribute to the development of over fifty illnesses including cancer and heart disease. One defense against free radicals is the antioxidants that help activate enzymes that reduce the impact of the radicals. Vitamins C and E, beta-carotene, and selenium appear to be important antioxidants. Appropriate daily amounts of vitamin C (200 mg), beta-carotene (6 mg), and selenium (55 mcg for women, 70 mcg for men) should be taken from red, yellow, and orange fruits and vegetables and green leafy vegetables. Scientists are not sure how these antioxidants work as supplements. The only way to feel secure about the effect of these elements is to get them in the form of food rather than supplements.

The exception to that suggestion is vitamin E. It is difficult to get the daily recommended amount of vitamin E from food. Subject to your doctor's advice, you might consider a vitamin E supplement. A daily intake of 200 mg of vitamin E produced a clear increase in the effectiveness of the immune system. Vitamin E may also help reduce the risk of heart disease.

The 1995 Health Professionals Follow-up research reported that the risk of prostate cancer might be reduced by a diet high in cooked tomatoes, like pasta sauce.

The American Journal of Epidemiology reported a study indicating that a diet high in foods containing vitamins C and E and the carotenoids that are contained in red, yellow, and orange fruits and vegetables reduces the risk of lung cancer.

PHYTOCHEMICALS

Researchers have identified a series of over 170 compounds in fruits, vegetables, grains, and legumes that are called "phytochemicals." They appear to inhibit the formation of some forms of cancer, improve the functioning of the cardiovascular system, and reduce cholesterol levels.

ALCOHOL

Some studies have shown that a moderate intake of alcohol can have a protective effect against heart disease. The phytochemicals in red wine might be the active ingredient. But for women, the risk of negative effects from alcohol may be great. The daily intake of even small amounts of alcohol appears to increase the risk of breast cancer, and the greater the intake, the higher the incidence of cancer.

Men should limit their intake of alcoholic beverages to one drink per day. Until the research results become clearer, women should avoid all alcohol or limit their intake to two or three drinks per week.

21 NUTRITIONAL STEPS THAT MAY HELP PREVENT CHRONIC DISEASES

1. Keep your intake of calories from saturated fat below 10 percent of your total calories.
2. Keep your total intake of calories from all types of fat below 30 percent of your total calories.
3. Get half your fat calories from monounsaturated fats like canola and olive oil.
4. Keep your daily intake of cholesterol below 300 mg.
5. Avoid foods that contain hydrogenated oils.
6. Get 400 mcg of folic acid each day from enriched breads and cereals, whole grains, oranges, orange juice, beans, and green vegetables.
7. Maintain an intake of vitamins B_6 and B_{12} from lean meat, poultry, seafood, and low-fat dairy products.
8. Take in 25 to 30 grams of fiber each day from whole-wheat products, bran, bulgar, oats, barley, legumes, fruits, and vegetables.
9. Drink eight cups of water each day.
10. Have at least five servings each day of fruits and vegetables.
11. Limit daily sodium intake to 2,400 mg.
12. Choose low-fat dairy products.
13. Increase your intake of fruits and vegetables that are high in potassium: potatoes, bananas, dried apricots, dates, oranges, orange juice, peaches, melons, pineapples, raisins, and strawberries.
14. Have two meals each week based on fish: salmon, tuna, halibut, turbot, sardines.
15. Take in 1,000 mg of calcium each day.
16. Get 200 to 600 IU of vitamin D each day.
17. Restrict your intake of lean red meat to two servings per week.
18. Have at least two servings per week of cooked tomatoes.
19. Men should limit their intake of alcohol to no more than seven drinks per week. Women should avoid all alcohol or limit their intake to three drinks per week.
20. Try and maintain your proper weight.

21. Realize that you will probably not be able to do all of the above all of the time, but the more you do, the better off you will be. Think of it as a sport and keep practicing.

WHAT'S GOOD TO EAT—MY WORKING LIST

Fruits
Apricots, dried
Apples
Red cherries
Cantaloupe
Orange juice (fortified with calcium)
Oranges
Strawberries
Bananas

Vegetables
Carrots
Leafy greens
Tomatoes
Sweet potatoes
Broccoli, fresh
Red peppers
Potatoes
Onions

Grains and Legumes
Whole-grain bread and pasta
Brown rice
Whole-wheat cereals
Dried beans (kidney)
Oatmeal
Bran
Lentils

Animal Proteins and Soy Products
Chicken or turkey breast, roasted, with skin removed
Sirloin steak, top round beef (4-ounce portions)
Lean pork (4-ounce portions)
Skim and low-fat dairy products
Soy products
Egg whites

Seafood
Tuna, canned in water
Halibut
Shrimp
Salmon
Sardines

Herbs and Spices
Paprika
Chili pepper
Parsley
Rosemary
Basil
Oregano
Garlic
Green tea
Ginger
Cinnamon

Supplements – I take:
Vitamin D – 400 IU
Calcium citrate – 1,000 mg
Vitamin E – 400 IU
Selenium – 200 mcg

SOUPS AND STEWS

Beaufort Stew

Chicken Souse Soup

Clam Chowder

Hearty Bean Soup

Minestrone alla Milanese

Pretzel Dumpling Soup

Red Onion Soup

Red Pepper Soup

Voodoo Gumbo

Charleston, South Carolina

AT the time of the American Revolution in 1776, Charleston, South Carolina, was the wealthiest, most beautiful and most sophisticated city in North America. It had the busiest port in the colonies and was often called "Little London." Today, you can walk through the historic streets of Charleston and get a clear sense of what early America looked like.

Cobblestone street, Charleston, South Carolina

Beaufort Stew

Makes 4 servings

The importance of removing bay leaves before serving. Bay leaves, which are also called laurel or bay laurel leaves, add a fragrant and delicate aroma and taste to a dish. They have a sharp central spine which, if eaten whole, could become stuck in the digestive tract. They are great for seasoning but not for eating. Remove bay leaves from all recipes before serving.

1 TO MAKE THE BROTH: In a 6-quart pot over high heat, heat the vegetable oil for a minute. Add the sausage and cook on all sides for a couple of minutes to brown. Add the garlic and cook for a minute, then add the broth, Old Bay seasoning, salt, and bay leaves. Bring the broth to a simmer and cook, uncovered, for 10 minutes.

2 TO MAKE THE STEW: Add the potatoes and simmer for 15 minutes, or until almost tender, then add the corn and simmer for a minute to heat through. Adjust the seasoning to taste. Add the tomatoes, then the crayfish and prawns (or shrimp) and cook for 4 to 5 minutes, or until the shellfish is just cooked through.

3 TO FINISH THE STEW: Strain the solids out of the liquid and transfer them to deep soup bowls. Garnish with sliced scallions and spoonfuls of the broth. (Eat the broth as is, or freeze it for another day to use as fish stock in a seafood stew or soup.)

Charleston Place Hotel, Charleston, South Carolina

1 tablespoon vegetable oil

1 pound smoked pork or turkey sausage, cut into ¾-inch rounds

5 cloves garlic, thinly sliced

3 quarts chicken or vegetable broth

2 to 3 tablespoons Old Bay seasoning

Salt to taste

2 bay leaves

6 new red potatoes, unpeeled, cut into 1-inch chunks

One 14-ounce can baby corn, drained

1 cup cherry tomatoes or chopped fresh tomatoes

2 pounds live crayfish and 8 freshwater prawns; or 3 pounds jumbo shrimp, in the shell

4 scallions, thinly sliced

The Food of the Bahamas

*W*HEN the first Europeans arrived in the Bahamas with Columbus in 1492, they found a group of people called the "Lucayans." The Lucayans were members of an Arawak tribe from South America and had been living in the Bahamas for about five hundred years. The Lucayans had learned to make large canoes and used them to cover the distances between the seven hundred islands that make up the Bahamas. Most of the Lucayans' food came from the sea—fish, shellfish, and turtle. And lots of conch, which is a local shellfish. The Lucayans made a primitive form of bread from the roots of plants and tried to practice a little farming.

Mural on the wall of the Junkanoo Museum, Nassau, The Bahamas

Burt Wolf

Chicken Souse Soup

Fat-free stock. How you store cans of beef or chicken stock can help you cut calories and lose weight. There is a substantial amount of fat in every can of stock. Place the cans of stock in the refrigerator overnight. The fat will congeal and you can spoon it off the top. You can save as much as 150 calories per can.

1. In a 4-quart saucepan over high heat, bring the chicken stock, allspice, and red pepper flakes to a boil. Lower the heat, cover the saucepan, then simmer for 10 minutes.

2. Add the garlic, onions, celery, carrots, and potatoes and simmer, covered, for 30 minutes more, or until the potatoes are tender.

3. Add the chicken and cook for 3 to 4 minutes, uncovered, or until the chicken is just cooked through. Season with salt and discard the allspice tied in cheesecloth. Remove the saucepan from the heat and add the lime juice, mint, and cilantro. Serve immediately.

Seagrapes Restaurant, Nassau, Bahamas

6 cups chicken stock

¼ cup whole allspice, tied in cheesecloth

½ teaspoon crushed red pepper flakes

4 cloves garlic, peeled and roughly chopped

1 cup finely diced onions

1 cup finely diced celery

1 cup finely diced carrots

2 cups peeled finely diced all-purpose potatoes

¾ pound skinless, boneless chicken breasts, cut into 1-inch squares about ¼-inch thick

Salt to taste

2 tablespoons fresh lime juice

2 tablespoons minced fresh mint

2 tablespoons minced fresh cilantro

Virginia Seafood

CAPTAIN John Smith, who was made famous by Pocahontas, noted in his Virginia diary that the fish were so thick he tried to catch them with a cooking pot.

Today, the watermen of Virginia harvest over eighty different species. One of the oldest harvests is for clams. Hundreds of years ago, the local tribes used clam shells as money. They felt that because of the purple streak on the inside of the shell, clams were particularly attractive and valuable.

Virginia watermen also bring in scallops. A scallop swims backward and can't see where it's going, even though it has fifty eyes. Sounds like parts of our government. The watermen also bring in oysters, which were one of the mainstays of the early colonial diet. There is a striped bass catch, and, of course, the ever popular, totally adaptable, and multitalented—soft-shell crab.

Clam Chowder

About clams. There are 2 major types of clams: hard-shell and soft-shell. Hard-shell, also known as quahogs, are named on the East Coast by size. The smallest are littlenecks, then top necks, then cherrystones, and then chowder or surf clams. Littlenecks, top necks, and cherrystones can all be eaten fresh on the half shell. The larger ones are better for chowder. The 8-inch wide geoduck clam of the Pacific Northwest is shelled, pounded, and served as geoduck steak.

Soft-shell clams are not good on the half shell. They can be used in chowder, but they are best steamed; hence their popular name "steamer clams." They can also be pulled from their shell, battered, and deep-fried.

All clams are a good source of iron, low-fat protein, and dietary fiber.

6 slices bacon, finely chopped

1 cup of finely chopped onions

¼ teaspoon paprika

3 cups cold water

3 cups potatoes, peeled and cut into ½-inch dice

½ teaspoon dried thyme

Three 6½-ounce cans chopped clams

1 cup half and half

Salt and freshly ground black pepper to taste

⅓ cup minced fresh parsley or chives for garnish (optional)

1   In a medium saucepan over medium heat, heat the bacon, covered, for a minute, or until some of the fat has rendered. Uncover the saucepan and continue to sauté, stirring constantly, for 2 minutes, or until a thin film of fat coats the bottom surface of the pan.

2   Add the onions and paprika, cover, and cook over low heat for 5 to 6 minutes, stirring on occasion. Add the water, potatoes, and thyme and bring the liquid to a boil.

3   Reduce the heat and simmer the soup, covered, for about 20 minutes, or until the potatoes are tender but not falling apart.

4   Add the clams with their juices and the half and half. Bring the soup just to a simmer and season with salt and pepper. Serve immediately, each portion garnished with parsley or chives, if desired.

Virginia Street Cafe, Urbanna, Virginia

Living Canteens

*A*LL life on our planet began in water—and so do we. It is our most essential nutrient. Without water our lives would end within days.

It's possible to think of plants and animals that live on land as canteens, trying to preserve water inside themselves. If you accept that, then it follows that the most difficult place for these plants and animals to survive is a desert. And only those plants and animals that are capable of very sophisticated adaptation are going to survive.

A stretch of terrain is described as a desert if it has less than ten inches of rain during a year. That means less water and more sun than any other area in the world. The primary job for the plants and animals of the desert is to hold on to the available water. Each develops its own strategy. Some of the results are quite strange; many are very beautiful.

One of the most common techniques for conserving water in the plant world is to become a *succulent*. Succulents develop root systems that suck moisture out of the earth. They also develop tissue that stores the water they collect. Cacti, yucca plants, and elephant trees are succulents.

Cacti, Baja California, Mexico

Hearty Bean Soup

About beans. Beans are the seeds of plants in the legume family. About a dozen major varieties have been grown for thousands of years. Beans are a rich source of iron and B vitamins and they are filled with valuable dietary fiber. One cup of beans supplies more fiber than equal amounts of celery, carrots, or rice. Four ounces of cooked dried beans have only about 115 calories.

When shopping for beans, remember that dried beans are much more nutritious, firm, and flavorful than canned or frozen beans.

1   In a large saucepan over moderate heat, heat the oil. Add the onions, garlic, and sausage. Cook, stirring often, for 6 to 8 minutes, or until the onions are tender.

2   Add the kale or escarole leaves. Cook for 5 minutes, stirring often, until the leaves are wilted. Add the chicken stock or water. Cover and simmer for 30 minutes, or until the leaves are tender.

3   Add the potatoes and beans, continue cooking for 25 minutes, stirring often, or until the potatoes are tender.

4   Transfer about a third of the soup to a blender or food processor fitted with a steel blade, and process until smooth. Return to the saucepan and stir to combine.

Baja California, Mexico

2 tablespoons olive oil

1 cup chopped onions

3 cloves garlic, minced

½ pound Polish kielbasa, linguiça, or similar sausage, cut into ½-inch pieces

8 cups fresh kale leaves or escarole leaves, washed well (about 1½ pounds)

6 cups chicken stock or water

3 medium all-purpose potatoes, peeled and diced

One 19-ounce can (2 cups) cannellini or white kidney beans, precooked, drained, and rinsed

The Four Seasons, Milano

*I*N 1987, the Four Seasons group purchased an eighteenth-century palazzo in the most fashionable district of Milan, and started converting it into a small hotel. As the construction got under way, the workmen discovered columns that looked considerably older than the palazzo. Then a fresco showed up that was clearly from the Renaissance. Within days, they realized that beneath the palazzo was a complete cloister that had belonged to a convent founded in 1428. The original plans for the building were given up. A new design was made and based on the ancient structure. The cloister became the center of the hotel. The lobby is the original chapel. The public and private rooms surround a garden that was modeled on fifteenth-century period drawings.

Everything about the hotel is quiet and restful, and the nuns would have enjoyed that aspect. But they were an order that avoided the comforts of life, so there's no telling how they would have responded to one of the most luxurious properties in Italy. Twenty-four-hour room service. Twenty-four-hour concierge service. A staff devoted to comforting their guests. A restaurant that has become a favorite of local food lovers as well as the residents of the hotel. It's quite possible that the nuns might have none of this. On the other hand, Saint Ambrose, the patron saint of Milan, was into the good life and he would have loved it. Especially the cooking.

Minestrone alla Milanese

1 In a large stock or soup pot over medium heat, heat ¼ cup of olive oil. Add the onions, leeks, celery, carrots, cabbage, green beans, and potatoes and stir for 2 minutes.

2 Add the prosciutto, zucchini, spinach, tomatoes, and tomato sauce and stir for another 2 minutes.

3 Add the chicken broth and bring to a boil. Lower the heat and simmer, covered, for 15 minutes.

4 Add the rice and beans, and simmer, uncovered, for 15 minutes, or until the rice is tender. Remove the soup from the heat.

5 In a small skillet, heat the 2 tablespoons of olive oil and sauté the rosemary for 30 seconds. Add this to the soup along with the parsley and cheese. Season with salt and pepper and serve immediately. Garnish with more cheese, if desired.

Four Seasons Hotel, Milan, Italy

¼ cup plus 2 tablespoons olive oil

1 cup finely chopped onions

1 cup finely chopped leeks, white and light green parts

1 cup finely chopped celery

2 cups finely chopped carrots

2 cups finely chopped cabbage (preferably Savoy)

1 cup green beans, cut into ½-inch lengths

2 cups boiling potatoes, peeled and cut into ½-inch cubes

½ cup finely chopped imported or domestic prosciutto

1 cup unpeeled zucchini, cut into ½-inch cubes

1 cup chopped fresh stemmed spinach, rinsed

⅔ cup chopped fresh or canned tomatoes

½ cup tomato sauce

6 cups chicken broth

¾ cup rice (preferably short-grain Arborio)

2 cups cooked dried (or canned) cannellini beans

1 tablespoon chopped fresh rosemary, or 1 teaspoon dried

¼ cup minced fresh parsley

½ cup grated Parmesan cheese, plus extra for garnish (optional)

Salt and freshly ground black pepper to taste

The Origin of the Pretzel

THE folklore of the pretzel says that it was developed by German monks as a symbol of arms folded in prayer and given to people as a reminder of the importance of praying. The word *pretzel* comes from an old Latin word meaning "little arms."

In Munich, pretzels are found everywhere and at all times, from an early morning breakfast to a late night snack. Usually, they are presented as a bread in a basket. In many restaurants the waitress will come to the table at the end of the meal and ask how many pretzels you have eaten, and add the appropriate amount to the bill. If you visit Munich, remember to keep track of your pretzel intake. There's a question period at the end of the meal.

Pretzel Dumpling Soup

1   TO MAKE THE DUMPLINGS: In a small saucepan over high heat, bring the milk to a boil with the butter and salt. Add the Cream of Wheat and pretzel crumbs, lower the heat, and stir with a small whisk, until the mixture thickens and begins to pull away from the sides and bottom of the pan.

2   Remove from the heat and transfer the batter to a mixing bowl. Add the scallions, parsley, and egg and set aside for 20 minutes. After 20 minutes, wet your hands in water and shape the batter into small rounds about ¾ inch in diameter.

3   In a large pot, bring the water, salted, to a boil. Add the dumplings, a few at a time, and simmer for 10 minutes, or until they're swollen and light. Remove them to a plate with a slotted spoon.

4   TO MAKE THE SOUP: Remove the mushrooms from the soaking liquid, reserving the liquid. Remove any tough stems that have not softened and chop the mushrooms. In a saucepan, add the stock and mushrooms to the reserved liquid and bring the liquid slowly to a simmer. Add the dumplings and reheat gently for 5 minutes, or until hot. Season with salt and pepper and garnish with the parsley. Serve immediately.

Hotel Rafael, Munich, Germany

For the Dumpling Batter:

¾ cup milk

1 tablespoon butter

Salt to taste

3 tablespoons Cream of Wheat

¼ cup pretzel crumbs (just process a few hard pretzels in a food processor)

2 tablespoons minced scallions

2 tablespoons minced fresh parsley

1 egg, lightly beaten

2 quarts water

For the Soup:

1 ounce dried mushrooms such as chanterelles or porcini, soaked in warm water until softened

5 cups beef stock

Salt and freshly ground black pepper to taste

¼ cup minced fresh parsley for garnish

Red Onion Soup

3 tablespoons vegetable oil

2 tablespoons unsalted butter

3 cloves garlic, peeled and thinly sliced,
    plus 2 large cloves peeled

2 pounds red onions, thinly sliced

¼ cup dry white wine

¼ cup balsamic vinegar

¼ cup flour

4 cups beef broth

4 cups chicken broth

½ teaspoon dried thyme

1 bay leaf

Long French baguette bread

Salt and freshly ground black pepper to
    taste

¼ cup cream (optional)

2 cups grated French Gruyère or Italian
    Parmesan cheese

1 In a 12-inch casserole or saucepan, heat the oil and butter. When the oil and butter are hot, add the sliced garlic and onions, and stir-fry for a minute. Cover and simmer, over low heat, for 15 minutes, stirring every 5 minutes to make sure the onions don't burn.

2 Add the wine and vinegar and cook for a minute to evaporate some of the alcohol. Add the flour and stir for a minute. Add the beef and chicken broths, thyme, and bay leaf, and over medium heat, bring to a boil. Whisk, cover, and simmer, over low heat, for 30 minutes.

3 Meanwhile preheat the oven to 350°F. Cut the French bread on the diagonal into sixteen ¾-inch-thick slices. Set them on a baking sheet and toast them in the oven for 20 minutes, turning them once, or until they're dried out. When dried out, rub each side of the bread slices with the peeled garlic.

4 Remove and discard the bay leaf from the soup and season it with salt and pepper. Stir in the cream, if using, and remove the soup from the heat.

5 Scatter some grated cheese on one side of the toasted bread and broil for a few seconds, or until the cheese is golden. Garnish each soup portion with 2 cheese-covered bread rounds.

Atlantis, Paradise Island, Bahamas

Red Pepper Soup

About bell peppers. Most bell peppers begin green and become red, sweeter, and more nutritious as they ripen. Bell peppers are very high in vitamins A and C.

For stuffing, large "fancy-style" bell peppers are best, but for cooking and salads, the "choice" grade is fine. Peppers should be firm and dark. Peppers that have been picked too early are pale, soft, and thin-skinned; overripe ones are dull. Avoid shriveled or wilted peppers. Take a good look at the stem side of the pepper—that's where decay usually starts.

1 TO PREPARE THE BELL PEPPERS: Cut a wafer-thin slice off the bottom of each pepper so it will sit straight on the plate. Slice the tops off each pepper and scoop out the seeds. Reserve the hollowed out peppers to hold the finished soup.

2 TO MAKE THE SOUP: In a 4-quart saucepan over moderate heat, heat the olive oil. Add the onions, cover, and simmer for 3 to 4 minutes, or until they've softened. Add the sweet potatoes, diced red bell peppers, chicken stock, thyme, and bay leaf and bring to a boil. Cover and simmer over medium heat for 25 to 30 minutes, or until the vegetables are tender.

3 TO FINISH THE SOUP AND SERVE: Strain the solids from the liquid and return the liquid to the saucepan. Discard the bay leaf. In a food processor or blender, puree the vegetables until they're smooth and return them to the liquid in the saucepan. Bring the soup to a simmer and season with salt and pepper. Ladle the soup into the hollowed-out peppers and garnish with the diced yellow or red bell peppers and a dollop of yogurt, if desired.

Manoir Richelieu, Charlevoix, Quebec

---

8 large red or green bell peppers, to use as serving containers for the finished soup, plus 1½ pounds red bell peppers, cored, seeded, and diced

2 tablespoons olive oil

1 cup finely chopped onions

1½ pounds sweet potatoes, peeled and cut into 1-inch cubes

6 cups chicken stock

½ teaspoon dried thyme

1 bay leaf

Salt and freshly ground black pepper to taste

½ cup finely diced yellow or red bell pepper for garnish (optional)

½ cup plain low-fat yogurt for garnish (optional)

Voodoo Gumbo

1 medium yellow onion, finely chopped

1 medium green bell pepper, seeded, cored, and finely chopped

3 medium stalks celery, finely chopped

8 tablespoons vegetable oil

½ cup flour

1 pound andouille sausage or kielbasa, cut into ½-inch dice

1 to 2 tablespoons "Cajun" or "Creole" seasoning (optional)

4 cups unsalted chicken stock

2 tablespoons Worcestershire sauce

1 cup chopped canned tomatoes

Two 15½-ounce cans pink or small kidney beans, drained

1 pound boneless, skinless chicken, cut into ¾-inch cubes

2 tablespoons hot sauce, or more to taste (optional)

1 cup sour cream (optional)

1 In a bowl, combine the onion, bell pepper, and celery, then remove ½ cup of the mixture and set aside for later.

2 TO MAKE THE BROWN ROUX: Over high heat in a small heavy saucepot, heat 6 tablespoons of the oil. When hot, add the flour, lower the heat, and stir constantly with a wooden spoon until the roux turns brown and smells nutty, 8 to 10 minutes. Remove the pot from the heat and immediately add the reserved ½ cup of vegetable mixture and continue to stir until the roux has cooled down. Transfer the roux, which is very hot, to a mixing bowl.

3 In a heavy 4-quart saucepan over medium heat, heat the remaining 2 tablespoons of oil. Add the remaining vegetable mixture and cook, stirring, for a couple of minutes. Add the sausage and "Cajun" or "Creole" seasoning, if using, cover, and cook over low heat for about 5 minutes, or until the vegetables are tender, but not brown.

4 Over medium heat, add the chicken stock, Worcestershire sauce, tomatoes, beans, and the reserved roux. Bring the liquid to a simmer and cook, uncovered, for 5 minutes. Add the chicken and cook for 5 minutes longer, or until the chicken is completely cooked through. Remove the pot from the heat and add the hot sauce if you like your gumbo hot and/or add the sour cream if you like it rich. Serve over rice.

Voodoo Cafe, Las Vegas, Nevada

SAUCES, DIPS, AND MARINADES

Blender Apricot-Yogurt Dressing

Honey Pico de Gallo

Low-Fat Dip for Vegetables

Mexican Salsa

Pico de Gallo

Red Chili Salsa

Rio Grande–Style Barbecue Marinade

Simple Horseradish Sauce

Lindblad's Special Expeditions

DURING the twenty-first century, tourism will be the biggest industry in the world. But in addition to the great cities and traditional tourist attractions, unusual and unspoiled destinations will become more and more important. The increase in the number of visitors to these unspoiled places could easily spoil them. One response to the problem has been the development of companies that are as responsive to the needs of the environment as they are to the expectations of the travelers.

One of the pioneers in this form of travel was Lars-Eric Lindblad. In 1958, he began taking travelers to places like Antarctica, the Galàpagos Islands, Mongolia, and Tibet.

I wanted to see what responsible expedition travel was like, so we headed off to the Baja Peninsula, off the west coast of Mexico, to board a ship called the *Sea Lion*. The *Sea Lion* belongs to Lindblad's Special Expeditions, a company that is run by Sven-Olof Lindblad, the son of the early pioneer.

I boarded the *Sea Lion* at the port city of La Paz, on the southern tip of the Baja. During the night the ship headed north through the Sea of Cortés.

I started the first day by watching the sunrise. A simple way to pass a few moments, but more than one passenger told me that watching the day begin filled them with a sense of connection to the natural rhythms of our planet. Only a few hours into the voyage and I understood what they meant.

About four and a half million years ago, forces inside the earth took a strip of land on the west coast of Mexico and pushed it off into the Pacific Ocean. That strip of land became the Baja Peninsula, and the water that came in and filled the 700-mile-long space between Mexico and the Baja is known as the Gulf of California, or the Sea of Cortés.

The Sea of Cortés has over fifty islands; most of them are uninhabited, and some are so remote that no one has bothered to give them names. There are upwellings of water behind many of the islands, and these surges bring nutrients up from the bottom. The nutrients attract fish, birds, and sea mammals. The fish, birds, and sea mammals attract tourists interested in nature.

The variety of conditions that exist in the Sea of Cortés has set up an ecosystem that supports a greater variety of sea life than any other similar-sized area in the world. Over 800 species of fish have been catalogued in the Sea of Cortés, and new ones are added each year.

James Wolf, kayaking, Baja California, Mexico

Blender Apricot-Yogurt Dressing

1 cup plain non-fat yogurt
¼ cup dried apricots, chopped
2 tablespoons vegetable oil
1 tablespoon honey
⅛ teaspoon dry mustard
Freshly ground black pepper to taste

About apricots. Apricots are a member of the plum family. They originated in northern China and were brought to Europe around 400 B.C. King Henry VIII's gardener brought apricots to England from Italy in 1542.

If you can't get apricots that are perfectly ripe and juicy, dried apricots are a good substitute. They are an excellent source of vitamin A, potassium, and iron, and can be soaked and pureed for use in puddings, and as a topping for ice cream.

1 In a blender, combine the yogurt and apricots and blend until smooth.

2 Add the remaining ingredients, blending until the mixture is well combined.

3 Chill until needed. Serve with grilled lamb and poultry.

Baja California, Mexico

About Honey

*T*HERE are more than three hundred varieties of honey in the United States, and the flavor of a particular honey depends on where the bees buzzed. The flower that the bee tapped will determine both the flavor and the color of the honey that the bee will be making.

In general, the lighter the honey the milder the flavor. But darker honeys have interesting flavors and that's why I use them. Honey can add flavor notes to seasonings, and to sauces and dressings.

Don't store honey in the refrigerator. Just keep it in a jar at room temperature. If it gets cloudy, which is part of the natural process of crystallization, heat it gently and it will return to its original liquid state. You can use a warm water bath or, after you make sure there's no metal on the container, you can put the jar in a microwave. A little stirring and the crystals will dissolve.

Honey Pico de Gallo

3 Roma tomatoes, seeded and finely diced

2 tablespoons minced onion

1 Haas avocado, peeled and cut into
    ¼-inch dice

1 fresh serrano or jalapeño pepper, seeded
    and minced

1 clove garlic, minced

Juice of 1 lime

1 tablespoon honey

Salt to taste

2 tablespoons minced fresh cilantro

About avocados. While the avocado is native to Central and South America, more avocados come from California than from any other part of the world. Their peak season is from January through April.

Avocados are highly digestible and provide vitamin A, several B vitamins, C, and E. There is a good amount of iron in avocados as well, and they are low in sodium. Avocados, however, are rich in fruit oil, which is a saturated fat. If you are on a low-saturated-fat diet (a good idea for most people), limit your intake of avocados.

Firm avocados can be ripened at home by leaving them in a sunny spot, or close them up in a paper bag and keep them in a warm place. Check their progress daily. Avocados bruise easily, so store them carefully and avoid buying ones that are bruised to begin with.

1 TO PREPARE THE TOMATOES: Core the tomatoes and quarter them, lengthwise. With a spoon, remove the juice and seeds and discard. Finely dice the remaining flesh and transfer to a bowl.

2 TO FINISH THE PICO DE GALLO: Combine the tomatoes with the onion, avocado, serrano or jalapeño pepper, garlic, lime juice, and honey. Season with salt and sprinkle the cilantro over the top.

3 Serve with meat, fish, and poultry.

La Mansion del Rio, San Antonio, Texas

Low-Fat Dip for Vegetables

About spinach. Spinach originated in Persia, now Iran. It was unknown in Europe until the Moors planted it during their invasion of Spain in the Middle Ages. A green leafy vegetable that is most closely associated with Popeye the Sailor and with little children who don't want to eat it, spinach is delicious when eaten raw or lightly cooked and horrible when it is overcooked. It is an excellent source of vitamin A.

Folacin, or folic acid, as it's sometimes called, is a vitamin that is found in green leafy vegetables such as spinach and is important to good health. Folic acid takes part in two of our essential body processes: It makes up genes and it helps form hemoglobin, the protein that carries oxygen throughout the body. Sufficient folic acid is also essential to a safe pregnancy. (Other good food sources of folic acid include wheat germ, dried beans and peas, and liver.)

There are two main types of spinach—smooth leaf, which usually ends up frozen, and crumpled leaf, which is usually sold fresh.

½ cup reduced-calorie or light mayonnaise

1½ cups plain non-fat or low-fat yogurt

4 scallions, chopped

¼ cup fresh lime juice

2 cloves garlic, minced

One 10-ounce package frozen chopped spinach, thawed, drained, and squeezed dry

Raw vegetables for serving

1 In a bowl, combine all of the ingredients except the raw vegetables.

2 Cover and refrigerate for 30 minutes to allow the flavors to blend. Serve with cut raw vegetables.

Baja California, Mexico

Mexican Salsa

4 large ripe tomatoes, peeled and coarsely
  chopped

½ cup finely chopped scallions

1 medium clove garlic, finely minced

¼ cup chopped fresh cilantro

1 (or more to taste) jalapeño pepper,
  trimmed, seeded, ribs removed, and
  finely chopped

1 teaspoon dried oregano, crushed

Juice of ½ lime

About scallions. Scallions, also called "green" or "spring onions," are adolescent onions, harvested before the bulb has a chance to develop. To buy the best scallions, look for those with crisp, green, unwithered tops and clean white bottoms. At home, cut off any brown tops or edges and store the scallions in a plastic bag in the refrigerator for not more than 5 days.

Many people find it difficult to chop scallions with a knife. Line up 2 or 3 scallions and place them on a cutting board. Holding them in a row with one hand, chop them into tiny rounds, going all the way into the dark green portion. Another technique is to take the bunch of scallions in one hand, and with clean, dry scissors, snip them into small pieces.

1 In a medium bowl, combine all the ingredients. Chill before serving.

2 Serve with chips or as a side sauce for meats, fish, and poultry.

Zarela's, New York City

Pico de Gallo

About coriander. Both the leaves and seeds of the coriander herb are used. The leaves are called "Chinese parsley" or "cilantro"; the seeds are called "coriander." The ancient Romans brought the herb back to Europe from the eastern Mediterranean. Its name comes from the Greek word for bedbug, because when the unripe seeds are bruised they give off a nauseating smell similar to that of the bug. Sugar-coated coriander seeds used to be served as candy in Scotland.

½ cup chopped scallions

1 fresh or canned jalapeño, serrano, or other hot pepper, finely chopped (adjust the amount of pepper for desired spiciness)

1 tablespoon vegetable oil

2 tomatoes, chopped

2 medium ripe avocados, pitted and chopped (optional)

Juice of 1 large lemon

6 sprigs cilantro, chopped

Salt and freshly ground black pepper to taste

1 In a small bowl, combine all the ingredients. Chill for 1 hour before serving.

2 Serve with chips or crackers or as a dip for vegetables.

San Antonio, Texas

Red Chili Salsa

4 cups tomato juice, preferably
    Sacramento brand

½ medium onion, finely diced

4 cloves garlic, minced

2 tablespoons chili powder

1 tablespoon red wine vinegar

1 medium red bell pepper, finely chopped

1 pound plum tomatoes, finely diced

2 tablespoons chopped fresh cilantro

1 bunch scallions, trimmed and
    thinly sliced

About garlic. Garlic has lived up to age-old claims of its benefits as a cardiac drug. Researchers have shown that eating garlic increases the amount of time your blood takes to coagulate, and reduces the blood levels of bad low-density lipid cholesterol, while boosting levels of the good high-density lipid cholesterol.

1 Place all the ingredients, except the cilantro and scallions, in a non-corrosive saucepan, and bring to a boil. Reduce to a simmer and cook, uncovered, for about 30 minutes. Add the cilantro and scallions and simmer for 10 minutes longer.

2 Use immediately or cool to room temperature and refrigerate.

3 Serve with beef and pork.

The Lucky Star, Virginia Beach

Rio Grande–Style Barbecue Marinade

Makes 2 cups

About Worcestershire sauce. The Romans were fond of a salted fish sauce called "garum." Worcestershire sauce is an anchovy-based meaty-tasting condiment that has its roots in this ancient Roman condiment. The modern version was developed by two English druggists, John Lea and William Perrins, who were given the recipe for a sauce by the British governor general of Bengal. They hated the sauce and poured it into a wooden barrel in their basement. Several years later they rediscovered the sauce, tasted it, and found they now liked it; they named it Worcestershire because it was made in the English district of Worcester.

Lea & Perrins Worcestershire sauce is still made the same way. Anchovies, soybeans, tamarind, vinegar, garlic, shallots, molasses, and spices are mixed and aged for 2 years in wooden vats. The sauce is pressed out, strained, and put in bottles.

One 8-ounce can tomato sauce
1 teaspoon dry mustard
1 teaspoon sugar
1 tablespoon Worcestershire sauce
1 tablespoon white vinegar
½ cup red wine
1 clove garlic, minced
Tabasco sauce to taste
½ cup vegetable oil

1 In a 2- or 3-quart saucepan, mix all the ingredients together. Simmer, uncovered, for 10 minutes.

2 Use as a marinade or basting sauce for meats and poultry.

San Antonio, Texas

Simple Horseradish Sauce

One 6-ounce jar white prepared
    horseradish

¼ cup non-fat plain yogurt, or more
    to taste

Salt and freshly ground black pepper
    to taste

About horseradish. Horseradish is the pungent root of a member of the cabbage family. It's called horseradish because it looks like a giant beige-colored radish. Native to southeastern Europe and western Asia, most of the horseradish grown in the United States comes from Illinois farm country, just across the Mississippi River from St. Louis.

Freshly ground horseradish has a much brighter and more pungent flavor than horseradish that has been preserved in vinegar.

1   In a bowl, mix all the ingredients together. Allow to sit at room temperature for 1 hour before serving.

2   Serve with seafood.

Las Vegas, Nevada

FISH AND SEAFOOD

Pan-Fried Catfish with Vegetables and Celeriac Sauce

Codfish Cakes

Cod Steaks with Tomato Sauce

Cod with Jarlsberg Sauce

Cod with Pesto Crust and Tomato Relish

Fish in Puff Pastry

Gravlax with Mustard Sauce

Fish with Eggplant

Halibut with Dill Cream Sauce

Grouper with Scales of Zucchini

Napa Crab Cakes

Monkfish with Two Sauces

Fish with Citrus Sauce

Oysters and Clams on Spinach

Red Snapper with Tomatoes and Olives

Salmon with Basil Crust and Ratatouille Salsa

Shrimp Stir-Fried with Snow Peas and Cashews

Shrimp with Three Mayonnaises

Willie's Crab Cakes

Soft-Shell Crab Sandwich

Spiced Sea Bass with Peppers and Mushrooms

Striped Bass

Tuna Cocktail

Wolfgang Puck's Grilled Tuna

Munich's Hotel Rafael

IN 1875, Stutzel's Ballhouse was built for debutante balls and concerts. And since then, it has been the focal point of Munich's social scene. Today, it is the Hotel Rafael and its owners have restored the rooms to their previous elegance. The furnishings are in a style called "Biedermeier," which was popular in Germany and Austria during the first half of the 1800s. Biedermeier was a character in a play who became a symbol of the responsible middle class. Biedermeier furniture is made from wood that is usually light in color. The design elements are drawn from Greek and Roman architecture, and there is always a meticulous attention to detail. The walls are covered with a collection of original prints and drawings, some dating back several hundred years.

One of the things that makes the hotel unusual is that it reflects Munich's unique balance between modern metropolis and Bavarian village. The rooms give you the feeling of a wealthy family residence. Some of the rooms have private terraces that look out over the city. There is a swimming pool on the roof with spectacular views. I was particularly impressed with the bathrooms. High ceilings, huge mirrors, marble all over the place, spacious showers, and oversized soaking tubs. You can even soak in the tub and look out at the skyline, and the place is so quiet, you'd never know that you were right in the middle of the Old City.

Pan-Fried Catfish with Vegetables and Celeriac Sauce

About Celeriac Sauce. Celeriac is a type of celery that is valued for its bulb shaped root. It is also known as knob celery and turnip-rooted celery and has been grown in England since the 1700s.

1   TO MAKE THE SAUCE: In a pot, bring the salted water to a boil with the slices of lemon. Peel and chop the celeriac with a stainless-steel knife (celery root oxidizes quickly when in contact with iron). Add the celery root to the water, and simmer, covered, over medium heat for 15 minutes, or until the root is tender.

2   While the celeriac is cooking, peel the carrots and cut them into ¼-inch dice; cut the zucchini into ¼-inch dice. With a slotted spoon, remove the cooked celeriac to a bowl and bring the water back to a boil. Add the carrots and boil, uncovered, for 1 minute; add the zucchini and continue boiling for 45 seconds. Drain the carrots and zucchini and reserve them for later.

3   In a blender or food processor, puree the cooked celeriac with the fish stock and cream and season with salt and pepper; transfer to a clean saucepan and over low heat bring back to a simmer. Season the sauce with lemon juice to taste.

4   TO COOK THE CATFISH: In a 10-inch skillet over medium heat, heat the oil and butter. Dredge the catfish in flour and shake off any excess. When the butter and oil are hot, add the fillets and sauté over medium heat, uncovered, for about 5 minutes per side, or until the fillets are cooked through.

5   While the fish is cooking in a pot, bring the cup of water to a boil. Add the carrots and zucchini and turn off the heat; this will reheat the vegetables without cooking them further.

6   To serve, remove the fish and blot off excess fat with a paper towel and set each fish fillet in the middle of a plate. Spoon the sauce around the fish. Drain the carrots and zucchini, pat them dry, and sprinkle over the sauce. Serve immediately.

Hotel Rafael, Munich, Germany

For the Sauce:

1 quart water, salted

2 slices lemon, peeled

1 medium celeriac (also known as celery knob or celery root)

2 medium carrots

1 small zucchini, washed and trimmed

1 cup fish stock or clam juice

1 cup heavy cream

Salt and freshly ground black pepper to taste

1 tablespoon or more fresh lemon juice

1 cup water

For the Catfish:

2 tablespoons vegetable oil

1 tablespoon butter

Six 8-ounce catfish fillets

Flour spread on a plate

Codfish Cakes

2 pounds all-purpose or Yukon Gold
    potatoes, peeled and quartered
Salt and freshly ground black pepper
    to taste
1 pound boneless cod
½ cup finely diced salt pork or bacon
    (4 slices)
¾ cup finely chopped onion
½ cup finely chopped celery
½ teaspoon dried sage
¼ cup flour for dredging
2 tablespoons vegetable oil
1½ cups tomato sauce
6 sprigs dill for garnish
6 lemon wedges for garnish

During the 1400s, when Portuguese sailors first fished the Grand Banks off the coast of Canada, they called the nearby island *Terra de Baccalaos . . .* which means "the Land of the Dried Codfish." These days, the island is known as Newfoundland. But if you spend time in any Newfoundland kitchen, you will quickly discover that it is still the land of dried codfish. And the most common way to prepare that fish is to make fish cakes.

1   In a pot of lightly salted water, boil the potatoes for about 20 minutes, or until they're tender. Drain and immediately mash them with a potato masher or fork. (Don't do this in a food processor or they will turn gluey.) Place the mashed potatoes into a mixing bowl, season with salt and pepper, and set aside.

2   In a separate pot of lightly salted water, simmer the fish for 5 minutes, or until the cod is just cooked through. Drain the fish and transfer to a plate. Allow the cod to dry while you prepare the seasonings.

3   Heat a medium saucepan and add the salt pork or bacon. Cook for 5 minutes or until the fat has rendered and the pork or bacon is golden. Add the onion and celery, cover, and cook over low heat for a few minutes, or until they're tender. Add the sage and transfer the mixture to the potatoes. With your fingers, flake the fish into the mixture and combine; adjust the seasoning.

4   Shape the mixture into 12 cakes about 2½ inches in diameter and ½ inch thick. Dip the fish cakes in the flour and shake off any excess.

5   In a large skillet, heat the vegetable oil over medium heat. Add the fish cakes and cook for 5 minutes on each side, or until they're golden brown. In a separate saucepan, heat the tomato sauce. Serve 2 fish cakes per person drizzled with tomato sauce, and garnish each portion with a sprig of dill and a lemon wedge.

Hotel Newfoundland, Newfoundland, Canada

Cod Steaks with Tomato Sauce

Makes 4 servings

About black pepper. Black pepper was first domesticated from its wild ancestor on the Malabar Coast of India. Pepper was the first Oriental spice brought to the West, and was a major foreign trade item for ancient Rome. At the time, pepper was worth more than its weight in gold.

When Christopher Columbus arrived in the West Indies, he thought he was in India. When he tasted a spicy dish that had been seasoned with chile, he wrongly jumped to the conclusion that it had been seasoned with pepper. The locals asserted the flavor was "chile" and Columbus said it was "pepper." The compromise name "chile pepper" stuck.

Pepper is actually a berry (called a "peppercorn") that turns black when dried in the sun. The strongest flavor is concentrated in the black skin. At the moment you break the kernel the flavor is at its peak, which is why freshly ground pepper is preferred by many chefs for dishes that are light in color.

4 cod steaks, about 8 ounces each
2 slices white bread, crusts removed
1 cup grated Jarlsberg cheese
2 tablespoons melted butter
Salt and freshly ground black pepper to taste
2 cups of your favorite tomato sauce

1   Preheat the oven to 400°F. Place the cod steaks on a baking sheet.

2   In a food processor, crumb the bread. Transfer the crumbs to a mixing bowl, combine them with the Jarlsberg and melted butter, and season with salt and pepper. Spoon some of this mixture over the cod steaks and bake for 15 minutes, or until the tops are golden and the fish is cooked through.

3   In a small saucepan over low heat, heat the tomato sauce. To serve, spoon some sauce on each dinner plate and place the cod steak over the sauce.

Kafe Gasa, Trondheim, Norway

Jarlsberg and the Viking Tradition

THE national cheese of Norway is Jarlsberg. It's a semi-soft, part-skim milk cheese with holes like Swiss cheese, but it is milder and it has a nuttier flavor. Jarlsberg makes their classic, but you can also get a hickory-smoked version and a Lite from which they have removed more than half the fat.

The cheese is named after Count Gustave Wilhelm Jarlsberg on whose estate it was first made. A cheese like Jarlsberg is very much in keeping with the gastronomic objectives of the Vikings. It is a simple and easy way to preserve the important nutrients in fresh milk. Preserved foods kept the Vikings alive during the winter and fed them during the long voyages that brought them throughout Europe and eventually to North America.

Cook House, open-air Folkmuseum, Trondheim, Norway

Cod with Jarlsberg Sauce

About nutmeg. Nutmeg is the inner kernel of the fruit from the nutmeg tree. Freshly ground nutmeg is more potent than powdered, but isn't always worth the effort.

There is a lattice-patterned skin on the surface of a nutmeg. When removed and ground, it is used as a seasoning called "mace."

2 tablespoons butter
2 tablespoons flour
1¼ cups milk
Salt and freshly ground black pepper to taste
Pinch ground nutmeg
¼ cup grated Jarlsberg cheese
¼ cup grated Parmesan cheese
Six 6-ounce boneless, skinless cod fillets

1 TO MAKE THE JARLSBERG SAUCE: In a 1-quart saucepan over medium heat, melt the butter. When the foaming subsides, add the flour and cook, stirring constantly with a wooden spoon, for 30 seconds. Remove the pan from the heat and gradually pour in the milk. Place the saucepan over medium heat and bring the milk slowly to a simmer, whisking as it comes to a simmer, and cook for a minute. Season with salt, pepper, and nutmeg and remove from the heat. Add the cheeses and stir until they melt into the sauce; reserve for later.

2 TO COOK THE FISH: Preheat the oven to 400°F. Set the cod fillets in a 9-x-13-inch baking pan and bake for 10 minutes, or until the fillets are just cooked through. Turn the broiler on to high, pour the sauce over the fish, and broil for 1 to 2 minutes, or until the sauce is golden brown and bubbling.
Serve immediately.

Kafe Gasa, Trondheim, Norway

Cod with Pesto Crust and Tomato Relish

1 cup prepared salsa

2 plum tomatoes, finely diced

1 tablespoon ketchup

¼ teaspoon liquid smoke (optional)

Salt and freshly ground black pepper
   to taste

2 slices white bread, broken into pieces

Six 8-ounce boneless, skinless cod fillets

⅓ cup prepared pesto sauce

About ketchup. Ketchup is believed to be Chinese in origin, and was first made with a base of mushrooms, rather than tomatoes. The Chinese word *Ke-tsiap* refers to the brine of pickled fish.

Today, ketchup usually has a spiced vinegar added to tomatoes. The grade of commercial ketchup is based on the percentage of tomato solids in the mix.

1 TO MAKE THE RELISH: In a medium bowl, combine the salsa, tomatoes, ketchup, and liquid smoke; season with salt and pepper and set aside for later.

2 TO COOK THE FISH: Preheat the oven to 400°F. In a food processor, crumb the bread. Set the cod fillets on a baking sheet and spread each fillet with some pesto sauce, then sprinkle with fresh bread crumbs. Bake for about 10 minutes, or until the fillets are just cooked through. Serve the relish on the side.

Radisson Hotel, Trondheim, Norway

Charlevoix, Quebec—Where the Locals Eat

CHARLEVOIX, like just about every other place in the world, has a series of down-home foods that are thought of as the "local stuff." And, as usual, there is a particular place with a reputation for preparing those foods authentically.

Allow me to present Chez Chantal. Conveniently located next to the train tracks and directly in front of the docks. In the early 1900s, a Native American woman used the building to sell baskets to tourists. Wishing to expand her product group, she began serving soup to the local dock workers and ice cream to the tourists.

In 1987, Simon Bouchard saw the potential of the food division and purchased the building. He dropped the basket line and concentrated on the snack food. Today Simon and his family run the business and it has become renowned among local gastronomes for two of the great lunch-counter dishes of Quebec. The first is *poutine*—crisp French fried potatoes that have just been made from scratch, carefully blended with small curds of soft, locally made farm cheese, then bathed in a rich gravy, and elegantly presented in a paper cup.

The second is *guedille*—strips of newly harvested lettuce, chunks of locally grown ripe tomatoes, ribbons of tender baked chicken, and all blended with a velvety mayonnaise and served in a delicately toasted hot dog bun.

Fish in Puff Pastry

2 sheets (one 17½-ounce box) frozen puff pastry, thawed

2 tablespoons olive oil

3 leeks, trimmed of 2 inches of dark green, finely chopped

Salt and freshly ground black pepper to taste

1 pound boneless Arctic char or salmon, cut into sixteen 1-ounce strips, each ¼ inch thick

1 egg, slightly beaten with 1 tablespoon water

24 asparagus tips with 1½ inches of stem

2 tablespoons butter

2 tablespoons minced shallots

¼ cup dry white wine

1 cup orange juice

1 cup chicken stock

Beurre manie: 2 tablespoons softened butter blended with 2 tablespoons flour

Pinch cayenne

1 TO PREPARE THE PASTRY: Unfold the thawed puff pastry sheets and cut each one into 4 squares.

2 TO MAKE THE FILLING: In a small skillet over low heat, heat the olive oil. Add the leeks and sauté for a minute to coat with the oil, cover, and simmer over low heat for about 10 minutes, or until they're softened. Season with salt and pepper and remove to a bowl. Heat a large non-stick skillet over medium heat. Sear the fish pieces for 15 seconds per side and remove to a plate.

3 TO ASSEMBLE THE FISH IN PASTRY: Line a baking pan with parchment or foil. Set 4 of the puff pastry squares on the baking pan. On each square, center 2 tablespoons of leeks, leaving a ½-inch border around the pastry unfilled. Top the leeks with 2 strips of fish, and build a second layer of leeks over the fish. Top the leeks with another strip of fish and cover with another square of dough. With a fork, press the edges of the dough together to form a seal. With a pizza cutter or knife trim the dough so the edges are even. Brush the top with the beaten egg mixture. With the tip of a knife, cut the center of each pastry package to let the steam escape. Refrigerate for at least 4 hours or up to 24 hours.

4 TO BAKE THE FISH: Preheat the oven to 425°F. Bake the fish in pastry for 35 to 40 minutes, or until the pastry is golden brown and the fish is cooked through.

5 TO MAKE THE GARNISH AND SAUCE: While the fish is baking in a pot of just enough water to cover, parboil the asparagus tips for 2 minutes, or until they are cooked but still firm. Drain and reserve. In a skillet, melt the butter and sauté the shallots until tender. Add the white wine and boil until almost evaporated. Add the orange juice and chicken stock and simmer until 1 cup remains. Whisk in the beurre manie in small bits and add just enough to thicken the sauce. Season with salt, and a touch of cayenne.

6 TO SERVE THE FISH: Spoon some sauce onto the center of each plate and center the fish in pastry in the middle. Scatter the asparagus tips around the pastry and serve.

Manoir Richelieu, Charlevoix, Quebec

Burt Wolf

Big Game Fishing

*B*IG game fishing, as a sport, got its start in western Europe in 1496 with the publication of the first book on the subject. The book was called *A Treatise on Fishing with an Angle.* Fishing with an angle meant fishing with a hook as opposed to a net or a spear or a harpoon. Gear in those days included a rod made of local wood, line that was made from braided horsehair, and a hook cast from iron.

In 1655, Izaak Walton wrote a book that became the most famous fishing book ever published. It is called *The Complete Angler,* and it introduced the idea of the reel. The basic equipment has changed very little over the years, although the materials and the construction techniques have taken advantage of our most modern technologies.

Boating became popular right after World War II, and big game fishing became the ideal activity to occupy the powerboater. The introduction of plastic made the gear lighter and stronger. Monofilament nylon line could withstand hundreds of pounds of pull and still be light enough for long casts.

Despite all these advantages, the angler still has to find the fish, a task which has become easier because of fish-finding sonar. The sonar has a radarlike device to search the bottom of the sea and send back a signal outlining the fish. Trolling from the boat allows the anglers to cover a large area of the sea and send their lines down to considerable depths.

But how big is a big-game fish? Recent records include a white shark at 2,600 pounds, a black marlin at 1,600 pounds, and a bluefin tuna at 1,500 pounds. The bluefin tuna is particularly impressive when you realize that that single fish was responsible for over 10,000 individual tuna sandwiches.

The Food of Hong Kong

*H*ONG KONG is a wealthy city. It has the world's third-highest per capita gross national product. It has the largest gold reserves in Asia. It has the largest per capita ownership of Rolls-Royce cars. It also has an appetite that goes along with its assets. Hong Kong is the world's largest importer of Cognac. It is one of the world's leading consumers of protein. And it has the world's highest per capita ratio of restaurants. In Hong Kong, there is one restaurant for every eight hundred people. Whatever it is that you want to eat or drink, Hong Kong will get it for you.

But when all of the fads and fashions of international gastronomy have been pushed to the back burner where they belong, and it's time to settle down to some good eating and drinking, Hong Kong's heart is Chinese and Hong Kong is home to some of the best Chinese cooking in the world.

The majority of the people who live in Hong Kong are of Cantonese heritage, and Canton is a part of China with an ancient reputation for good food. The Cantonese kitchen is based on fresh foods of high quality that are prepared in ways that preserve their original appearance and natural flavors: barbecued meats . . . minced beef and egg flower soup . . . crabmeat and sweet corn soup . . . steamed shrimp . . . pan-fried boneless chicken with lemon sauce . . . baked salted chicken . . . sautéed diced chicken with chile . . . grouper fillet with a sweet corn sauce . . . and broccoli with crabmeat.

Gravlax with Mustard Sauce

For the Gravlax:

3½ pounds fresh salmon, center cut

*2 large bunches fresh dill, washed and
    patted dry*

¼ cup kosher salt

¼ cup sugar

2 tablespoons crushed black pepper

For the Mustard Sauce:

8 tablespoons olive oil

2½ tablespoons white wine vinegar

2½ tablespoons prepared mustard

½ teaspoon salt

½ teaspoon white pepper

¼ cup sugar

Pinch ground cardamom (optional)

1   TO MAKE THE GRAVLAX: Ask the fish dealer to cut the salmon in half, remove the backbone and small bones, and leave the skin on.

2   In a glass or enamel rectangular dish, set half of the salmon, skin side down. Place the dill over the fish. In a small mixing bowl, combine the salt, sugar, and pepper, then sprinkle this mixture evenly over the dill. Set the other salmon half, skin side up, over the dill.

3   Cover the fish with plastic wrap and place a baking sheet on it that is larger than the dish which contains the fish. Set weights, such as heavy cans, on the baking sheet and refrigerate the salmon for up to 3 days, turning the fish over every 12 hours and basting it with the liquid which accumulates in the bottom of the dish. After basting, replace the weights each time.

4   TO FINISH AND SERVE: Remove the salmon from the marinade and discard the dill and seasonings. Pat the fish dry and set it skin side down on a cutting board. Cut wafer thin slices on the diagonal and away from the skin. Serve with the mustard sauce.

5   TO MAKE THE MUSTARD SAUCE: In a medium bowl, combine all of the ingredients and blend thoroughly. Cover the sauce and place in the refrigerator for at least 2 hours before serving. Before serving, beat with a whisk or fork.

Bryggen Restaurant, Trondheim, Norway

The Seafood of Norway

*T*HE Vikings who settled here were great fish eaters, and Trondheim is still a good town for a fish lover. As a matter of fact, all of Norway is into fish. The nation has a very large fishing industry and exports some of the finest fish in the world.

Norway does its traditional fishing in the rich grounds of the Arctic Ocean. The waters are cold and clean. But Norway also pioneered Atlantic salmon farming. They offer salmon fresh, frozen, smoked, and cut up into convenient shapes. Norwegian fishermen are always trying to make life easier for the cooks. They also have a big catch of cod which feeds primarily on krill that gives the cod a sweet, mild flavor and a firm, white flesh. And Norwegians are very serious about their haddock.

Norwegian salmon with friends, Trondheim, Norway

Fish with Eggplant

2 teaspoons cornstarch

2 egg whites

*1 pound fillet of grouper, cut into
1-x-3-inch strips*

*½ to 1 cup vegetable oil,
plus 1 tablespoon*

*2 cups unpeeled eggplant, cut into
1-x-3-inch strips*

1 tablespoon sesame oil

2 medium cloves garlic, sliced

4 teaspoons minced peeled ginger

1 dried red chile pepper (optional)

1 teaspoon Chinese chili sauce

½ tablespoon soy sauce

*1 teaspoon cornstarch dissolved in
1 tablespoon water*

Salt to taste

½ cup chopped fresh cilantro for garnish

*2 scallions, white and green parts, thinly
sliced, for garnish*

About eggplant. Eggplants originated in China and India, where they have been grown for thousands of years. They are called eggplants because the early varieties were small and egg-shaped. Eggplants are available year-round, and can be baked, broiled, sautéed, stuffed, or fried. A small eggplant can be cooked whole, and often has a better flavor than the large ones.

1   In a bowl, combine the cornstarch and egg whites and marinate the grouper in this mixture in the refrigerator for 1 hour.

2   Set a strainer or colander over a bowl. In a large skillet or wok, heat the ½ to 1 cup vegetable oil until very hot. Stir-fry the eggplant for 30 seconds, and with a slotted spoon transfer the eggplant to the strainer. Add the fish to the oil and stir-fry for 1 minute. Transfer the fish to the strainer.

3   Carefully pour the oil into a bowl and cool. Clean the wok and return it to high heat. Heat the sesame oil with the tablespoon of vegetable oil in the wok and stir-fry the garlic, ginger, chile pepper, and chili sauce for 30 seconds.

4   Return the fish and eggplant to the pan and stir-fry for 30 seconds.

5   Add the soy sauce and dissolved cornstarch and boil for a minute. Season with salt. Serve immediately and garnish with cilantro and scallions.

The Regent, Hong Kong

Halibut with Dill Cream Sauce

Makes 4 servings

About dill. Dill is most widely known as the seed that gives dill pickles their flavor. Though native to Asia, dill is now grown the world over. Medicinally, small amounts of dill have been used as a mild tranquilizer to help infants sleep.

1 Season the halibut steaks with salt and pepper and set them in a skillet just large enough to hold them in a single layer. Cover the fish with water and bring the water to a simmer over medium heat. Simmer, partially covered, for 4 to 5 minutes, or until the fish turns opaque and is just cooked through. If the fish is cooked before the sauce is done, keep it warm, in the water, off the heat.

2 While the halibut is cooking, in another saucepan, melt the butter and sauté the shallots for a minute, or until tender. Add the wine and boil down until 2 tablespoons remain. Add the fish stock or clam juice and simmer until ¾ cup remains.

3 Blend the cornstarch into the cream and stir this into the simmering stock. Bring the mixture to a boil and simmer over low heat for a minute, or until thickened. Season with Worcestershire sauce, lime juice, and dill.

4 Remove the steaks from the water and pat them dry. Serve with the sauce.

Legend of the Seas, *Cruising Alaska*

Four 6-ounce halibut steaks
Salt and freshly ground black pepper to taste
1 tablespoon butter
¼ cup minced shallots or onions
½ cup white wine
1 cup fish stock or bottled clam juice
2 teaspoons cornstarch
¾ cup light cream
Worcestershire sauce to taste
2 teaspoons fresh lime juice
¼ cup minced fresh dill

Grouper with Scales of Zucchini

2 medium (1 pound) zucchini, scrubbed
   clean

4 cups water

2 tablespoons olive oil

1 medium onion, finely chopped

One 28-ounce can plum tomatoes
   with juices

Salt and freshly ground black pepper
   to taste

1 teaspoon chopped fresh thyme
   or ½ teaspoon dried

10 medium fresh basil leaves

Four 8-ounce skinless, boneless fillets of
   grouper, wolf fish, or orange roughy

½ cup dry white wine

About zucchini. Zucchini is a summer squash. Like all squashes, it originated in South and Central America and was introduced to Europe during the years of colonization in the sixteenth and seventeenth centuries. Zucchini was brought back to America in 1921 by Italian immigrants, who had a special fondness for the soft tender vegetable.

When buying zucchini, look for slender ones that are 3 to 6 inches long. At this size, the seeds are edible and the flesh is sweet. The skin should be smooth and unblemished and either dark green or light green with dark strips. Zucchini will last in the vegetable bin of the refrigerator for 2 to 3 days.

1   Cut the zucchini into slices ⅛ inch or thinner. In a large pot, bring the water to a boil, add the zucchini, and boil for 2 minutes. Drain, run under cold water to stop the cooking, pat the slices dry, and set aside.

2   TO MAKE THE SAUCE: In a saucepan over medium heat, heat the olive oil. Add the onion and cook over low heat for 3 to 4 minutes, uncovered, or until the onion is soft. Add the tomatoes with their juices, salt and pepper, the thyme and the basil leaves. Simmer over medium heat, uncovered, for 10 minutes.

3   Preheat the oven to 300°F. Season the fish fillets with salt and pepper and place them in a non-stick sauté pan large enough to hold them in a single layer. Arrange the zucchini slices over the fish, forming an overlapping pattern that looks like the scales of a fish. Add the wine and more salt and pepper to taste and bring the wine to a simmer. Cover with a lid or foil and transfer to the oven. Bake for 10 minutes, or until the fish is flaky.

4   While the fish is cooking, blend the sauce into a smooth puree.

5   To serve, ladle some sauce over the entire surface of a dinner plate. Remove the zucchini-covered fish with a slotted spatula to a paper towel to absorb any excess liquid before setting it in the middle of the sauce.

Romora Bay Club, Harbour Island, Bahamas

The Romora Bay Club/Eleuthera

*T*HE water taxi from Eleuthera crosses the harbor in four minutes and ends up at the dock of the Romora Bay Club. There are thirty-eight small houses on the property, lots of local vegetation, a few tennis players, and a very laid-back main lounge. As a matter of fact, the whole place is laid-back and quiet. Rosie and Goldie, the parrots, are the two noisiest guests, and fortunately they have a very limited vocabulary.

Grouper with Scales of Zucchini, Romora Bay Club, Harbour Island, The Bahamas

Napa Crab Cakes

2 medium tomatoes

4 ounces scallops, chilled

⅓ plus ½ cup heavy cream

½ teaspoon salt, plus extra to taste

Freshly ground black pepper to taste

1 pound cooked fresh lump crabmeat,
   cleaned to remove any shell

1 medium bunch fresh chives, finely
   chopped

1½ cups chopped canned tomatoes

About scallops. Scallops are delicate, sweet shellfish that are found in 4 varieties in the coastal waters of the United States. The largest is the sea scallop, about the size of a walnut, which is found in deep water. Bay scallops, especially Peconic Bay scallops fished on Long Island, are very sweet and succulent and are about the size of a small finger joint. They are extremely rare. Small bay scallops or calico scallops are the size of lima beans and are fished off the Carolina coast. One of the only varieties of scallop served in the shell is the pink scallop found near Seattle. These are about the same size as Peconic Bay scallops.

Scallops are called *coquilles St. Jacques* in French. Legend has it that Saint James the Apostle (Saint Jacques) saved a bridegroom from the sea. The bridegroom was covered with scallop shells and the scallop became a symbol for Saint James.

Nutritionally, scallops contain 100 calories per ½-pound serving. They are low in fat, and high in protein and calcium.

1   Preheat the oven to 350°F. Butter a baking sheet.

2   Cut the tomatoes in half, horizontally. With a spoon, scoop out the interior with the juices and seeds and discard. Cut the remaining tomato shell into ⅛-inch dice.

3   In a food processor, puree the scallops. Through the feeding tube, slowly drizzle the ⅓ cup of heavy cream into the food processor as you continue to process. When the puree is smooth, season it lightly with salt and pepper. Transfer the mixture to a large bowl.

4   Gently fold in the scallop mixture with the crabmeat, half the fresh tomatoes, and half of the chives, then season with the ½ teaspoon of salt.

5   Shape the mixture into 12 small disks, about 2 inches wide and ½ inch thick and set them on the baking sheet. Bake for 15 minutes, or until cooked through.

6   TO MAKE THE SAUCE: While the crab cakes are cooking, in a
    small skillet, bring the canned tomatoes and ½ cup of cream to
    a simmer for a couple of minutes. Season to taste with salt and
    pepper and remove the sauce from the heat.

7   To serve, spoon some sauce in the middle of each plate, and
    set 3 crab cakes on top. Sprinkle the remaining tomatoes and
    chives over the sauce and crab cakes and serve immediately.

Napa, Las Vegas, Nevada

Makes 6 servings

Monkfish with Two Sauces

One 16-ounce jar pickled beets, drained

One 14.5-ounce can chicken broth

One 10-ounce package frozen "petite" peas, thawed

¼ cup heavy cream

2 pounds boneless monkfish, cut into 2-inch square pieces

6 tablespoons melted unsalted butter, plus 1 tablespoon unmelted

1 tablespoon paprika

Salt and freshly ground black pepper to taste

About paprika. Paprika is a dark red, powdery seasoning that is made from dried sweet red peppers. Like all members of the Capsicum pepper plant, paprika was first grown in Central America and brought to Europe after Columbus. Paprika took hold in Hungary, where it is an essential ingredient in goulash and paprikash. Paprika is sweet, not hot, and it adds color as well as taste to food. Like wine, this seasoning has different styles and flavors. The best have a true essence of sweet red pepper and a hint of smokiness.

In Spain, paprika is known as *pimentón*. It is used extensively in paella and chorizo, a Spanish pork sausage. The best Spanish paprika is grown on the Mediterranean coast in the province of Murcia.

1 TO MAKE THE SAUCES: In a food processor or blender, puree the beets with 1 cup of the chicken broth and set aside in a small saucepan. Puree the peas with the remaining broth and the heavy cream and set aside in another saucepan.

2 TO PREPARE THE MONKFISH: Preheat the oven to 400°F. Dip each piece of monkfish in the melted butter. Sprinkle each piece with paprika and set on a baking sheet. Roast for 10 minutes, or until just cooked through.

3 While the monkfish is roasting, in separate saucepans, over low heat, simmer the beet and pea sauces. When they come to a simmer, season each one with salt and pepper. Blend a tablespoon of butter in the beet sauce and remove both sauces from the heat.

4 TO SERVE: Center 3 pieces of monkfish in the middle of each plate. Spoon about ⅓ cup beet sauce to the left of the fish and ⅓ cup of pea sauce to the right.

Restaurant Havfruen, Trondheim, Norway

Fish with Citrus Sauce

Makes 6 servings

About parsley. Fresh parsley is the most available, useful, and nutritious of all the herbs. Parsley can be kept in a airtight container for a week in the refrigerator. It is very high in vitamin C.

There are 2 main types of parsley. Curly leaf, the most common, has tight, compact curled leaves that should be separated from the stems, which are often bitter. Italian, or flat-leaf, parsley is more pungent than regular parsley.

Chinese parsley is not parsley at all. It is the immature greens of the coriander spice plant. It resembles parsley but has quite a different and distinctive flavor.

½ cup orange marmalade

2 tablespoons bottled white horseradish

3 teaspoons minced garlic

¼ cup chopped fresh parsley

½ teaspoon Tabasco sauce

2 tablespoons fresh lime or lemon juice

½ cup pineapple juice

2 tablespoons dark rum or Cognac (optional)

¼ cup vegetable oil

½ teaspoon salt

Freshly ground black pepper to taste

Six 8-ounce boneless, skinless fillets of grouper, or 6 sea bass or salmon steaks

1 In a non-corrosive saucepan, combine the marmalade, horseradish, garlic, parsley, Tabasco sauce, lime or lemon juice, pineapple juice, rum or Cognac (if using), and oil. Season with salt and pepper and marinate the fish in this mixture for 1½ hours.

2 Preheat your grill or broiler. Remove the fish from the marinade and transfer the remaining marinade to a small saucepan and bring it to a simmer. Grill the fish for 3 to 5 minutes per side, depending upon the thickness. Baste the fish as it cooks with the marinade. Serve the fish with a tablespoon or so of the marinade.

The Great Abaco Beach Resort, Abaco, Bahamas

Food in Colonial Virginia

*W*HEN the first English colonists arrived in Virginia in 1607, the waters were filled with seafood and the forest with game, fruits, vegetables, and nuts. The land could have supplied the settlers with all the food they needed, and yet they were starving to death.

There were two major reasons for the devastation. First, the settlers were uninterested in eating anything they had not eaten back in England. A deadly idea. And second, most of the colonists to Virginia came from the middle class. They were tradesmen and merchants, not skilled at farming or hunting. But with more than a little help from the local natives who traded with the settlers and taught them about corn, many of the colonists survived, and eventually learned to farm.

By the middle of the 1600s, Virginia's main crop was tobacco. It was extremely profitable and led to the development of the plantations. The tobacco plantations were built along Virginia's rivers. Ocean-going ships tied up at the plantation's private dock, tobacco was loaded on to them for export and goods that were purchased in England were unloaded—furniture, art, clothing, and food. At first the planters preferred to import much of their food rather than give up a tobacco field.

But by the late 1600s, things changed. Virginia developed its own style of cooking, a style that was based on local food products, with particular interest in seafood, Smithfield hams, fresh fruits and vegetables, and peanuts.

Oysters and Clams on Spinach

Makes 4 appetizer servings

1 In a bowl, soak the spinach in several changes of water until it's completely free of grit; set aside for later.

2 In a 4-quart saucepan, set a vegetable steamer over 2 inches of water and bring the water to a boil. Add the clams to the steamer, cover, and steam for 5 minutes, or until they open. Remove the clams from their shells and reserve for later.

3 In a 12-inch skillet over low heat, cook the bacon until it begins to render its fat. Increase the heat to medium and cook the bacon until it is crisp. Discard the fat in the skillet and add the butter to the remaining cooked bacon bits in the skillet. Over medium heat, heat the butter. Add the shallots and sauté for 3 to 4 minutes, stirring on occasion, or until tender.

4 Add the vermouth to the shallots and boil until almost evaporated. Hold a strainer over the skillet and strain the oysters' juices into the skillet. Reserve the oysters for later. Simmer the juices until almost evaporated.

5 Add the spinach to the skillet, cover, and cook for a minute or until just wilted. Season with salt and pepper. Add the oysters and clams you reserved to the spinach and cook them, uncovered, for 30 seconds, or until the edges of the oysters curl.

6 With tongs, set some spinach on 4 appetizer dishes. Place 3 oysters and 3 clams per person on top of the spinach, then spoon the skillet juices and bacon bits over the shellfish and spinach. Serve immediately.

Lemaire Restaurant, Jefferson Hotel, Richmond, Virginia

1 1/2 pounds fresh spinach, stemmed

12 hard-shell clams

4 slices bacon, finely chopped

2 tablespoons butter

1/4 cup minced shallots

3 tablespoons dry Vermouth

12 oysters, opened by fishmonger, juices reserved

Salt and freshly ground black pepper to taste

Red Snapper with Tomatoes and Olives

1 teaspoon minced garlic

½ cup olive oil

¼ cup lemon juice

*Salt and freshly ground black pepper
    to taste*

Six 7-ounce red snapper fillets

1 shallot, chopped

*4 tomatoes, peeled, seeded, and coarsely
    chopped*

*⅔ cup sliced pitted Kalamata or other
    large Italian, French, or Greek black
    olives*

15 large leaves fresh basil, finely shredded

½ cup packed fresh parsley, chopped

Vegetable oil spray

About Florida Tomatoes. Florida tomatoes are shipped just before they are fully ripe. That helps keep them in good condition during the trip, but when you see a Florida tomato in your market it may still have a pink color.

When you get them home, do not put them in the refrigerator; the cold stops the ripening process and kills the flavor. Let the tomatoes ripen at room temperature for two or three days until their red color deepens, and they will be ready to eat.

If you let other fruits like pears or bananas sit next to a ripening tomato, the tomato will ripen even faster. And always keep your tomatoes stem side up. The area around the stem is very delicate and easily damaged. You don't want the weight of the tomato to rest on that surface.

1   In a mixing bowl, combine half the minced garlic with half the oil, the lemon juice, and salt and pepper. Marinate the fish in the mixture at room temperature for an hour, turning once.

2   In the bowl of a food processor, chop the shallot, tomatoes, olives, basil and parsley. Transfer to a bowl, add the remaining olive oil, and season to taste with salt and pepper; set aside.

3   Preheat the oven to 350°F. Spray a large skillet with vegetable spray. Heat the skillet over medium heat and sauté the fish for 2 minutes a side or until opaque throughout. Remove the skillet from the heat and with a wide spatula, transfer the fish to a baking dish.

4   Top the fish with the tomato mixture and bake for 10 to 15 minutes, or until the interior of the fish is opaque and cooked through. Remove and serve with the pan juices over rice, pasta, or potatoes.

Edgewater Beach Hotel, Naples, Florida

Salmon with Basil Crust and Ratatouille Salsa

Makes 6 servings

About basil. Basil is a deep-green plant with 2-inch long glossy leaves. Thinly chopped fresh basil leaves strewn over fresh tomatoes and drizzled with olive oil make a delicious summer dish, popular in the south of France and in Italy. Basil leaves are the main ingredient in the Genovese specialty, pesto sauce.

Basil originated in ancient India, where this herb was said to be sacred to the gods Vishnu and Shiva. The ancient Greeks, Romans, and Hebrews believed that basil had the power to give great strength.

¼ cup olive oil

½ cup finely diced onion

1 cup finely diced red bell pepper

2 cups finely diced eggplant

½ teaspoon minced garlic

One 28-ounce can plum tomatoes, drained and chopped

1 cup finely diced zucchini

¼ teaspoon dried thyme

Salt and freshly ground black pepper to taste

2 slices white bread, broken into pieces

¼ cup (packed) fresh parsley, minced

¼ cup (packed) fresh basil, minced

Six 8-ounce boneless, skinless salmon fillets

1   TO MAKE THE RATATOUILLE SALSA: In a medium skillet over medium heat, heat the olive oil. When hot, add the onion, bell pepper, eggplant and ¼ teaspoon of garlic and sauté for 2 minutes, or until the vegetables are tender. Add the tomatoes, cover, and simmer over low heat for 10 minutes, or until they're tender. Add the zucchini and thyme and simmer, covered, for 5 minutes. Season with salt and pepper and set aside for later.

2   Preheat the oven to 350°F. In a food processor, crumb the bread, then combine it with the remaining ¼ teaspoon of garlic, the parsley, and basil.

3   TO BAKE THE SALMON: Set the fillets on a baking sheet, season them lightly with salt and pepper, and spread some of the basil bread mixture on top. Bake for 10 minutes, or until they're just cooked through.

4   TO SERVE: Center a piece of salmon in the middle of a plate and spoon some of the ratatouille salsa on the side.

Radisson Hotel, Trondheim, Norway

71

Shrimp Stir-Fried with Snow Peas and Cashews

1¼ pounds raw medium shrimp, peeled and deveined

½ teaspoon salt, plus extra to taste

2 teaspoons cornstarch

1 egg white

1 tablespoon dry white wine or vermouth

8 ounces snow peas or sugar snap peas

¼ cup peanut or vegetable oil

1 clove garlic, finely chopped

½ cup chicken stock

One 8-ounce can sliced bamboo shoots, drained

1 tablespoon soy sauce

2 tablespoons oyster sauce

1 teaspoon sugar

2 tablespoons cornstarch mixed with ¼ cup cold water

1 cup unsalted cashews

Freshly ground black pepper to taste

Cooked rice for serving

About thickening agents. Cornstarch is a common thickening powder that is made from lightly refined dried corn. Oriental cooks use cornstarch to thicken sauces and as a batter coating for deep-frying. American bakers use cornstarch as a thickener for fruit pies.

A frequent substitute for cornstarch is arrowroot, which is the dried and powdered root of the arrow plant. The American Indians used arrowroot to heal wounds caused by poison arrows.

When making the substitution, use 1 tablespoon arrowroot for every 2½ tablespoons cornstarch. Tapioca flour is another thickening substitute for cornstarch. Tapioca flour is the powder made from the dried ground root of the Brazilian cassava plant.

Cornstarch, arrowroot, and tapioca flour will break down and lose their thickening properties if they are cooked too long. When using cornstarch in puddings, custards, and pie fillings, use a double boiler and follow the recipe instructions carefully to avoid overcooking.

1 TO MARINATE THE SHRIMP: Season the shrimp with the ½ teaspoon of salt. In a small mixing bowl, with a fork, combine the cornstarch with the egg white and wine. Add the shrimp, toss well to combine, cover, and marinate for 1 hour in the refrigerator.

2 In a medium pot, bring the salted water to a rapid boil, drop in the peas, and cook for 30 seconds. Drain them and run them under cold water to stop the cooking process. Pat dry. Measure out the remaining ingredients.

3 TO COOK THE SHRIMP AND SNOW PEAS: Set a 12-inch wok or skillet over high heat for 30 seconds. Add the oil and swirl it around the pan and heat for another 30 seconds. Add the shrimp and stir-fry for 10 seconds. Add the garlic and stir-fry for 5 seconds, then add the chicken stock, snow peas, and bamboo shoots and bring the liquid to a simmer. Add the soy sauce, oyster sauce, and sugar and bring the liquid to a boil

again. Add the cornstarch/water mixture to the skillet and stir. Bring to a simmer and cook until thickened. Add the cashews and remove from the heat. Season to taste with salt and pepper. Serve over rice.

Restaurant Mask, Las Vegas, Nevada

Shrimp with Three Mayonnaises

2 cups prepared mayonnaise

½ cup diced fresh mango

2 tablespoons water

¼ teaspoon minced garlic

1 teaspoon chili powder

¼ teaspoon ground cumin

Salt and freshly ground black pepper
    to taste

18 jumbo shrimp, peeled and deveined

¼ cup flour, spread on a plate

3 tablespoons vegetable oil

6 Boston lettuce leaves, washed and dried

About mayonnaise. Mayonnaise has been made in the countries around the western Mediterranean Sea for hundreds of years. It's named after the town of Mahón, on the island of Minorca in the Spanish Balearic Islands. The Spanish say mayonnaise was invented there, but the French say they created the sauce and named it after a French naval victory near the port of Mahón.

Mayonnaise in its most basic form is a thick mixture of egg yolks and oil, which thickens as the oil is incorporated into the yolks. Technically, mayonnaise is an emulsification. The Spanish and French use olive oil, but any good vegetable oil or a blend of oils will do.

1   TO MAKE THE MAYONNAISES: In a blender, process ½ cup of mayonnaise with the mango and water and puree until smooth. Transfer to a small bowl. In another small bowl, blend the garlic with ¾ cup of mayonnaise, and in a third small bowl combine the remaining ¾ cup mayonnaise with chili powder and cumin. Season each with salt and pepper, cover, and set aside in the refrigerator for later.

2   TO PREPARE THE SHRIMP: Lightly coat each shrimp with flour and shake off any excess. In a large skillet over medium heat, heat the vegetable oil. When hot, add the shrimp and sauté for 2 minutes per side, or until they just turn pink. Cover the skillet and simmer the shrimp over low heat for another 3 minutes, or until they are just cooked through.

3   TO SERVE: Set 3 shrimp on a piece of lettuce and spoon a dab of each type of mayonnaise on the side of each portion.

Restaurant Havfruen, Trondheim, Norway

Willie's Crab Cakes

About tabasco. In 1868, Edmund McIlhenny planted a small crop of red peppers on a little island off the coast of Louisiana. When he harvested the peppers, he cut them up, mixed them with vinegar and salt from a dome under the island, and aged the mix in wooden barrels. Once aged, he stored the mixture in old cologne bottles. A year later, he shared some with his neighbors, who encouraged him to market the spicy sauce. He called it Tabasco, after a small river in Mexico. Today, Edmund's grandchildren manufacture and sell over 450,000 two-ounce bottles of Tabasco sauce each day.

8 ounces finely chopped cooked shrimp

8 ounces lump crabmeat, cleaned and picked over to remove any bits of shell

2 teaspoons Dijon-style mustard

¼ cup mayonnaise

2 tablespoons minced fresh parsley

2 teaspoons Worcestershire sauce

½ teaspoon Tabasco sauce

2 teaspoons bottled white horseradish

Salt to taste

Cayenne to taste

⅛ teaspoon Cajun spice mix (optional)

1 egg

2 tablespoons dried bread crumbs

1½ cups crushed potato chips, for dredging

2 tablespoons vegetable oil, or more, for frying

1   In a large bowl, combine all the ingredients but the potato chips and vegetable oil.

2   Form the mixture into twelve 2-x-½-inch round cakes and pat the crushed potato chips on both sides of the crab cakes.

3   In a large non-stick skillet over medium heat, heat the oil and sauté the crab cakes for 2 to 3 minutes on each side, or until they're golden and hot throughout.

Timbuktu, Virginia Beach, Virginia

Soft-Shell Crab Sandwich

¼ cup prepared mayonnaise

2 tablespoons prepared barbecue sauce

¼ teaspoon minced garlic

¼ cup flour

Salt and freshly ground black pepper to taste

4 soft-shell crabs (have fishmonger clean them)

2 tablespoons vegetable oil

1 tablespoon butter

4 Kaiser rolls, split in half

8 leaves of lettuce, washed and dried

Slices of ripe tomato (optional)

Soft-Shell Crabs. Soft-shell crabs were eaten during colonial times, but the eaters were all local to the catch. Soft-shells need to be eaten shortly after they are caught, before they turn back into hard shells. The first commercial shipping of soft-shell crabs took place in 1870, after the development of the railroads. The crabs were sent to Philadelphia. The national distribution of soft-shells began with the sophisticated refrigerated-transport of the 1940s.

1   In a small bowl, combine the mayonnaise with the barbecue sauce and garlic and set aside. In a shallow bowl or on a plate, combine the flour with the salt and pepper.

2   Pat the crabs dry with paper towels. In a 12-inch skillet over medium heat, heat the oil and butter. As the oil is heating up, dip the crabs in flour, on both sides, and shake off any excess.

3   Sauté the crabs, shell side down, over medium heat, for 3 to 4 minutes, averting your face from the skillet as the crabs begin to cook because they spatter like a volcano (after a few minutes the sputtering settles down).

4   With tongs, turn the crabs over and cook for another 3 to 4 minutes, or until they're slightly red and firm. Spread both sides of the roll with barbecue mayonnaise, set lettuce and tomato (if using) on one side of the bread, top it with a crab and the other half of the roll.

Virginia Street Cafe, Urbanna, Virginia

Spiced Sea Bass with Peppers and Mushrooms

Makes 4 servings

About mushrooms. Most edible fungi are called "mushrooms." There are close to 2,000 varieties. The word *mushroom* stems from the Teutonic word for moss, *mousse.* After the Norman invasion, the English began calling these fungi "mushrooms." In France, they are called *champignons,* after the French word for "field," *champs.* The Italians simply call them *funghi.*

1   Preheat the oven to 400°F. In a small mixing bowl, with a fork, combine the allspice, cumin, cinnamon, cayenne, and salt. Rub ½ teaspoon of this mixture onto each side of the fish and set aside. Combine the remaining spice mixture with the bread crumbs.

2   Set the fish on a baking sheet, and top each portion with about 1 tablespoon of the seasoned bread crumbs. Drizzle some of the melted butter over the bread crumbs and bake for 10 to 15 minutes, or until the flesh just flakes. Do not overbake.

3   TO MAKE THE SAUCE: While the fish is baking, in a medium skillet over medium heat, heat the oil. Add the peppers and mushrooms and sauté, stirring, for a minute. Add the water or stock, cover, and simmer for 3 minutes, or until the peppers are wilted but still have some texture. Stir in the barbecue sauce and remove from the heat.

4   TO SERVE: Center the fish in the middle of each plate and spoon some peppers and mushrooms around each portion.

Buzio's, Las Vegas, Nevada

¼ teaspoon each ground allspice, ground cumin, and ground cinnamon

⅛ teaspoon cayenne

½ teaspoon salt

Four 8-ounce sea bass fillets or steaks

¼ cup dry bread crumbs

2 tablespoons melted butter

2 tablespoons olive oil

2 medium red bell peppers, seeded, cored, and cut into ¼-inch dice

4 ounces mushrooms, trimmed, wiped clean, and cut into ¼-inch dice

2 tablespoons water or chicken stock

1 tablespoon favorite prepared barbecue sauce

Striped Bass

2 navel oranges, peeled of skin and white
  pith

1 bunch watercress, stems removed,
  leaves only

Four 6-ounce fillets of striped bass

1 cup vegetable broth

½ cup dry white wine

1 cup chicken broth, preferably reduced
  sodium

2 fresh tomatoes, peeled, cut in half,
  juices squeezed out, and finely
  chopped

4 scallions, trimmed and thinly sliced

4 to 6 leaves of Napa cabbage, white core
  removed, thinly shredded

Salt and freshly ground black pepper
  to taste

1 cup thawed frozen peas

1 With a sharp paring knife, cut in between the membranes of
   the oranges to loosen the segments.

2 Choose wide soup bowls in which to serve this dish and scatter
   some orange segments and watercress leaves in the bottom of
   each soup bowl; reserve for later.

3 Preheat the oven to 375°F. Set the fish fillets in a baking pan
   and cover them with ¼ cup of the vegetable broth. Cover the
   baking pan with aluminum foil and bake for 20 minutes, or
   until the fish is just cooked through.

4 While the fish is cooking, in a 3-quart saucepan, boil the white
   wine over medium heat until 2 tablespoons remain. Add to the
   wine the remaining ¾ cup of vegetable broth, the chicken
   broth, tomatoes, scallions, and shredded cabbage and simmer
   for 2 minutes; season with salt and pepper. Remove the
   saucepan from the heat and reserve until the fish is cooked
   through.

5 Remove the fish from the oven and keep it loosely covered
   while you finish the broth. Bring the broth back to a simmer
   and add the peas; simmer for 30 seconds. Set a fish fillet in the
   bottom of each soup bowl and ladle the broth and vegetables
   over the top; serve immediately.

Lemaire Restaurant, The Jefferson Hotel, Richmond, Virginia

Tuna Cocktail

About cinnamon. Cinnamon is the dried bark of a tree that is native to Ceylon and parts of southern India. The cinnamon tree is a deep green evergreen that has leaves and blossoms like the orange tree, and a papery bark like a cork or birch tree. In biblical times, cinnamon was used as perfume.

1   TO MAKE THE TOMATO MARMALADE: In a non-reactive 9-inch skillet, bring the tomatoes, sugar, red wine vinegar, garlic, and cinnamon stick to a hard boil. Reduce the heat to medium and simmer for 15 to 20 minutes, or until almost all the liquid has evaporated. About ½ cup will remain and the mixture will look syrupy. Discard the cinnamon stick, season with salt and pepper, and cool to room temperature.

2   TO MAKE THE TUNA: In a broiler or stove-top grill over high heat, cook the tuna for 3 to 5 minutes per side or until charred on both sides, depending on the thickness of the tuna and the degree of doneness you prefer. Remove and cool completely. When completely cool, cut into ¼-inch dice, combine with the mayonnaise, and season with salt and pepper.

3   TO MAKE THE AVOCADO LAYER: Right before serving, peel, pit, and cut the avocados into ¼-inch dice. In a bowl, combine the dice with the lemon juice, olive oil, and cilantro, and season with salt and pepper.

4   TO ASSEMBLE THE COCKTAIL: Layer the ingredients in eight martini glasses or 6-ounce wineglasses beginning with the tuna layer in the bottom of the glass, followed by 1 tablespoon of the tomato marmalade and topped with the avocado on top. In each glass, stick a thin strip of red pepper in the center of the cocktail. Take a very thin apple slice, core the side of the slice, make a small incision in the center and place the slice on the edge of the glass for garnish.

The Ritz-Carlton, Naples, Florida

1 pound (4) ripe plum tomatoes, peeled and chopped

2 tablespoons sugar

¾ cup red wine vinegar

1 clove garlic, minced

1 cinnamon stick

Salt and freshly ground black pepper to taste

1 pound tuna steak

¼ cup mayonnaise

2 ripe Haas avocados

¼ cup lemon juice

2 tablespoons olive oil

½ cup finely chopped fresh cilantro

8 red pepper strips, 2 inches long and ¼ inch wide

8 thin slices of unpeeled apple for garnish

Wolfgang Puck's Grilled Tuna

1 onion, thinly sliced

1 small eggplant, peeled and thinly sliced

4 tablespoons olive oil

1 tomato, chopped

2 cloves garlic, minced

1 tablespoon plus 1 teaspoon chopped
    fresh basil; or 1¼ teaspoons dried,
    crushed

1 cup cooked corn kernels

Salt and freshly ground black pepper
    to taste

1½ tablespoons red wine vinegar

Two 1-inch-thick pieces fresh tuna,
    about 1¼ pounds

Fresh mint leaves for garnish

About corn. Corn originated as a gigantic grass growing on the slopes of the Andes of South America. The cultivation of corn, which dates back over 3,000 years, marked the end of the nomadic lifestyle for many Indian tribes.

Corn is a good source of carbohydrates and fiber. Yellow corn is rich in vitamin A. An average corn ear has about 90 calories.

As soon as a corncob is picked, the sugar in the kernels starts turning into starch, so the sooner you eat the corn after picking, the sweeter it will taste. It is best stored refrigerated.

Look for fresh green husks, and tight rows of kernels. Avoid corn with dry or discolored stems, or very large (overripe) kernels.

1 TO MAKE THE VEGETABLES: Brush both sides of the onion and eggplant slices with 2 tablespoons of the olive oil. Sauté in a large non-stick sauté pan, or grill for 3 minutes on each side. If using a sauté pan, you may have to do this in several batches. Chop the onion and eggplant and toss together with the tomato in a medium mixing bowl. Add the garlic, 1 tablespoon fresh basil, corn, and salt and pepper. Add 1½ tablespoons of olive oil and the vinegar and toss to combine. Set aside.

2 Brush the tuna with the remaining ½ tablespoon of olive oil and season with freshly ground pepper and the remaining teaspoon of basil. Sauté in a large sauté pan over high heat for 2 to 4 minutes per side, depending on the thickness of the fish and the degree of doneness you prefer. Slice the tuna into ¼-inch-thick slices.

3 Arrange the vegetables in the center of each plate and top with the tuna slices fanned out. Garnish with fresh mint.

Spago's, Hollywood, California

POULTRY

Bahamian Grilled Chicken

Banana Stuffed Chicken

Chicken and Cauliflower with Pecorino Romano

Chicken and Red Peppers

Chicken Braised in Beer with Belgian Endive

Chicken Cacciatore

Chicken Breasts with Walnut Sauce

Chicken Stovies with Clapshot

Chicken Carino

Chicken Waterzooi

Chicken with Citrus Sauce

Greek-Style Chicken

Chicken with Macadamia Nuts

Jerk Chicken with Mango Relish

Pecan-Crusted Chicken

Grilled Chicken with Sweet Potato Sauce

Great Abaco Beach Resort, Bahamas

*T*HE Abacos are one of the world's great centers for yachtsmen and many of the resorts are designed for people who sail up as well as drive up. The Great Abaco Beach Resort is a good example. The resort is half hotel and half marina. The marina contains 185 slips with hookups for fresh water, electricity, telephone, television, and what appears to be the most essential facility for yachtsmen—a laundry! Yachts from all along the east coast of North America pull into the resort to relax and unwind after their passage to the Bahamas. They also use it as their home port as they travel through the Bahamas.

The hotel property is spread out over twenty-three acres of beachfront. Most of the rooms are set into villas that have been placed just above the shore. There's a pool, an outdoor bar, and all the other amenities that are normally associated with a tropical resort. Plus a very pleasant hotel staff who are interested in doing what they can to help you relax.

Bahamian Grilled Chicken

About thyme. After parsley and sage, thyme is the most commonly used herb in the world. Thyme is native to the rocky slopes around the Mediterranean and was first used for its medicinal value. The Greeks and the Romans cooked with thyme and extracted its aromatic oil to use in perfumes.

Fresh thyme has a wonderful bitter tang and whole branches are often used in a marinade for meats to be grilled outdoors.

4 chicken breast halves, skin on, bone in

Salt and freshly ground black pepper to taste

Juice of 2 fresh limes or 1 lemon

2 tablespoons vegetable oil

¼ cup finely diced bacon

½ cup finely chopped onion

½ cup thinly sliced green bell pepper strips

½ cup finely chopped celery

2 cups diced canned tomatoes and their juices

1 cup chicken stock

1 tablespoon Worcestershire sauce

½ teaspoon dried thyme

1   TO GRILL THE CHICKEN: Season the chicken with salt and pepper and marinate in lime or lemon juice for 10 minutes. While the chicken is marinating, heat the grill. Grill for 10 minutes on each side or until the breasts are just cooked through. Keep the skin on as you grill the chicken to keep it moist. You can take the skin off after cooking. While the chicken is cooking, make the sauce.

2   TO MAKE THE SAUCE: In a 2-quart saucepan over medium heat, heat the oil and bacon. When the bacon is brown, add the onion, green pepper, and celery and cook, covered, over low heat for 10 minutes, or until the vegetables are tender.

3   Add the tomatoes and their juices, the chicken stock, Worcestershire sauce, and thyme and simmer, uncovered, for 10 minutes. Season with salt and pepper.

Great Abaco Beach Resort, Bahamas

Rum Point

RUM POINT appears to have gotten its name as the result of a ship that wrecked on the nearby reefs. The ship was carrying a cargo of rum. After the wreck, barrels of rum floated ashore. When they were discovered by the local residents, they also got wrecked. These days, there are a number of bars and restaurants on Rum Point that will help you re-create the experience.

The History of Duty-Free Shopping

The idea of duty-free shopping goes back for thousands of years. One of the easiest ways for a king to pick up a few extra dollars was to place a tax on luxury goods coming into his country. That tax was added to the retail price of the product and everybody paid for it—what we now call an import duty. One of the easiest ways to avoid the import duty was to do your shopping on the high seas, ship to ship, or maybe on a little island that didn't have a tax agent. Eventually, the kings decided to let sailors buy luxury goods like tobacco and alcohol without paying the duty. The theory was that they were going to use those products in an area that was not part of the king's territory, so let's give 'em a break.

The modern duty-free business got started just after World War II, when a duty-free shop was opened at Ireland's Shannon Airport. The Irish government did not charge an import duty on the goods that were being sold to the passengers. And the duty-free shop passed on those savings to the purchaser. In 1948, airlines began selling duty-free liquor and tobacco onboard their flights. Today, duty-free shops are found at virtually every international airport, border crossing, cruise ship, international flight, and in-port towns where the nation has come to understand how profitable this business can be.

top left: *The Valley of Fire State Park, Nevada*
top right: *Chocolate Brownie with Ice Cream and Kahlúa, Las Vegas, Nevada*
above: *Shrimp Stir-Fried with Snow Peas and Cashews, Las Vegas, Nevada*
left: *Drive-up wedding chapel, Las Vegas, Nevada*

PHOTOS BY BURT WOLF

above: *Spoonbread, Richmond, Vir*
top left: *Shirley Plantation, Vir*
middle left: *Shirley Plantation, Vir*
left: *Richmond, Vir*
PHOTOS BY BURT

left: *Jerk Chicken with Mango Relish, Naples, Florida*
below: *Crabmeat Salad, Naples, Florida*
PHOTOS BY BURT WOLF

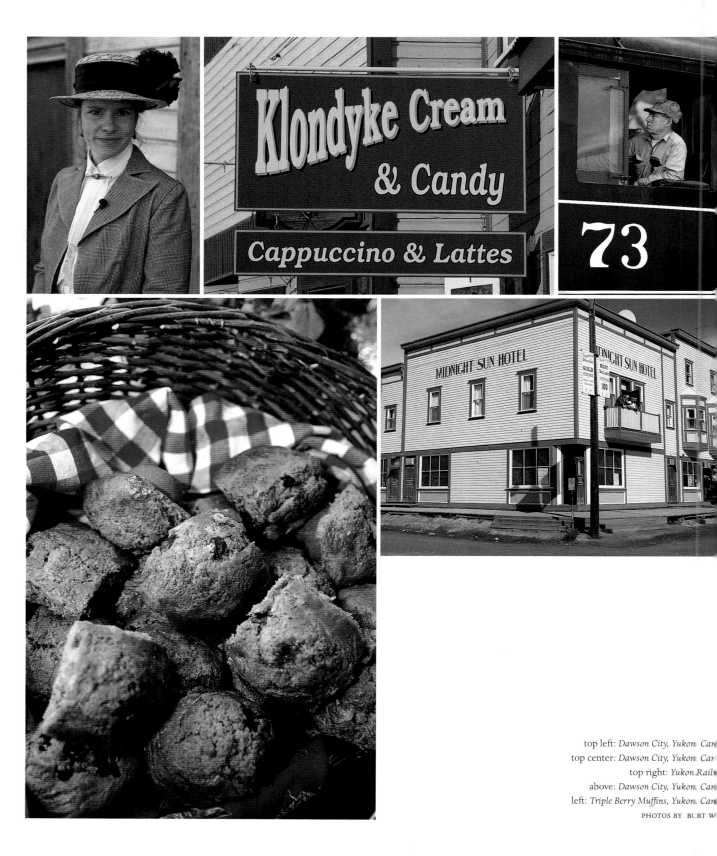

top left: *Dawson City, Yukon, Can*
top center: *Dawson City, Yukon, Can*
top right: *Yukon Rail*
above: *Dawson City, Yukon, Can*
left: *Triple Berry Muffins, Yukon, Can*

PHOTOS BY BURT W

left: *Petty Harbor, Newfoundland, Canada*
bottom left: *Figgy Duff, Newfoundland, Canada*
below: *Newfoundland, Canada*
PHOTOS BY BURT WOLF

top left: *Cranberries, Baja California, M*
above: *Pears, Baja California, M*
middle left: *Copper pots, Baja Califo*
M
far left: *Grapes, Baja California, M*
left: *Cactus, Baja California, M*
PHOTOS BY KURT V

left: *Deserted island, Baja California, Mexico*
top right: *Garlic, Baja California, Mexico*
above: *Preserved food, Baja California, Mexico*

PHOTOS BY BURT WOLF

above: *The Bah*
top left: *The Bah*
middle left: *Bahamian Lamb Curry, the Bah*
bottom left: *The Bah*
PHOTOS BY URT

Banana Stuffed Chicken

About bananas. The banana originated in India and Southeast Asia and is one of the oldest fruits cultivated by man. In many parts of the tropics, banana is a staple starch crop and it is eaten in place of rice or bread. Banana plants were brought to North Africa, the Canary Islands, the West Indies, and the Americas in the fifteenth and sixteenth centuries.

There is often confusion about bananas because they are also known as plantains. For American purposes, bananas are sweet yellow-skinned fruits (they are actually berries). Plantains are the nonsweet green-skinned fruits that are part of West Indian and Hispanic cuisine. Plantains are larger than yellow bananas, and should be cooked, either boiled or fried.

4 boneless, skinless chicken breast halves, tenderloins removed

Salt and freshly ground black pepper to taste

2 small ripe bananas, peeled and halved

2 tablespoons butter

2 tablespoons minced garlic

1 tablespoon minced shallots

1 Granny Smith apple, peeled and diced

1 tablespoon curry powder

3 tablespoons flour

2½ cups chicken broth

¼ cup flour for dredging

1 egg, beaten with 2 tablespoons milk

½ cup dry bread crumbs

2 tablespoons vegetable oil

¼ cup light cream (optional)

2 cups cooked long-grain rice

4 cilantro sprigs for garnish

1   TO PREPARE THE CHICKEN *(see Note):* Cut the chicken breast halves almost in half again and open them up like a book so you form a butterfly shape. Place a piece of plastic wrap over the chicken and, using a heavy skillet or mallet, pound them to even out their thickness and make them thin. Lightly salt and pepper each chicken breast. Enclose a piece of banana by folding up the ends and sides around the banana and rolling up the chicken. Wrap each stuffed chicken piece in plastic and refrigerate for an hour or more.

2   TO MAKE THE SAUCE: In a saucepan, heat the butter and sauté the garlic and shallots for a minute, or until they're soft. Stirring with a wooden spoon, add the apple, curry powder, and flour and cook for a minute. Slowly whisk in the chicken broth and simmer for 15 minutes. Season with salt and pepper.

3   TO COOK THE CHICKEN: Preheat the oven to 450°F. Lightly dredge the chicken in the flour, beaten egg, and bread crumbs, making sure each chicken piece is entirely coated with bread

(continued)

NOTE: An alternate way of making this dish, without stuffing the chicken with the banana, is to bread the chicken cutlets and cook them in a skillet. Before serving, set some slices of banana under the cooked chicken and spoon the curry sauce around it.

crumbs. Heat the oil in an ovenproof skillet and sauté the chicken on all sides to brown. Transfer the skillet to the oven and bake, uncovered, for 15 minutes, or until the chicken is just cooked through.

4   TO FINISH THE SAUCE: While the chicken is cooking, puree the sauce in a food processor or blender until the sauce is smooth. Pass it through a sieve and transfer it to a small saucepan. Add the cream if you wish, and simmer over low heat until hot. Season with salt and pepper.

5   TO SERVE THE CHICKEN: Mound some cooked rice in the middle of each plate. Slice the chicken into ¾-inch slices and set the slices around the rice. Ladle the sauce around the chicken. Garnish each plate with a sprig of cilantro.

Rum Point Club Restaurant, Cayman Islands

Chicken and Cauliflower with Pecorino Romano

About cabbage and cruciferous vegetables. We've known for a long time that cabbage is a good source of dietary fiber and vitamin C. Now we are learning that cabbage is also high in beta-carotene, a building block for vitamin A. Scientists believe that eating cabbage may help prevent cancer. In fact, all the vegetables in the cabbage clan—broccoli, Brussels sprouts, and cauliflower—have been found to help the body's defense system. These vegetables are called "cruciferous" vegetables because they have a crosslike structure at their base or stem.

4 tablespoons olive oil

2 whole boneless, skinless chicken breasts, split and cut into ½-inch pieces

¼ teaspoon freshly ground black pepper

1 small head cauliflower, cored and trimmed into florets

1 medium onion, thinly sliced

¾ pound mushrooms, trimmed and sliced

1 bunch scallions, cut into 1-inch pieces

1 tablespoon cornstarch dissolved into ½ cup chicken stock or water

3 cups cleaned spinach leaves

Grating of Pecorino Romano cheese for garnish

1   In a large skillet or wok over medium-high heat, heat 2 tablespoons of the oil. Add the chicken pieces, sprinkle with the pepper, and stir-fry the pieces for 2 to 3 minutes or until they are lightly browned. Remove the chicken from the pan and set aside.

2   To the same skillet, add 1 more tablespoon of oil and heat. Add the cauliflower and onion and stir-fry for 6 minutes. Cover and cook for 5 minutes more. Remove and set aside.

3   Add the last tablespoon of the oil and heat. Add the mushrooms and scallions and sauté for 4 minutes. Return the chicken, cauliflower, and onion to the pan and add the cornstarch mixture. Continue cooking, covered, until the cauliflower is tender and the chicken is cooked, about 5 minutes.

4   Arrange the raw spinach leaves on a serving platter and spoon the chicken and cauliflower over the spinach. Garnish with a grating of Pecorino Romano cheese.

Rome, Italy

Chicken and Red Peppers

2 chicken breasts, bone in, skin off, split

½ teaspoon salt

½ teaspoon freshly ground black pepper

1 teaspoon flour

2 tablespoons vegetable oil

1 cup thinly sliced onions

4 bay leaves

½ cup white wine, water, or chicken stock

2 cups chopped fresh tomatoes

1 cup chicken stock

One 7-ounce jar roasted peppers, drained and cut into 1-inch pieces (1 cup)

About onions. Botanically, onions are members of the same family as lilies and daffodils. They were first grown for food in the Middle East. The Spaniards brought them to the Americas and now billions of pounds are grown in the United States each year.

There are dozens of types of onions. But the most common are the yellow or white Globe onions, which have a strong aroma and a firm, crisp texture. These are the best all-purpose onions for cooking, stewing, and frying. The large sweet red onion, Bermuda, Vidalia, and Maui onions are better for salads and sandwiches.

Onions not only taste good but they are good for you. Doctors in ancient Greece and in the Far East used onions to treat a variety of ills. Now, modern science is discovering that onions may help prevent high blood pressure, heart attacks, and stroke. There is a chemical in onions that helps raise your body's high-density lipids, or "good" cholesterol level. This keeps your blood flowing freely, reducing the chance of fat buildup in the veins and hardening of the arteries. Perhaps the tradition of cooking high-cholesterol meats such as liver with onions is in response to body knowledge. A doctor at Tufts University in Boston has used onions to treat patients with high cholesterol levels.

The hotter the onion the better for your health. Tangy yellow and white onions are more beneficial than mild red onions.

Buy onions as you need them and store them in a cool, dry place. Look for onions that are hard and firm, with no soft spots or green sprouting tips; the flatter the base the better the taste.

1 Season both sides of the chicken breasts with salt and pepper. Sprinkle the breasts with flour.

2 In a large skillet over medium-high heat, heat the oil. Sauté the chicken breasts about 5 minutes on each side, or until they're golden. Add the onions and bay leaves. Cook for 2 minutes, or until the onions are wilted. Add the wine, water, or stock and

stir to loosen bits on the bottom of the pan. Stir in the tomatoes and cook for 2 minutes. Stir in the chicken stock and cook for 10 minutes, stirring often, until the chicken is fully cooked.

3 Transfer the chicken pieces to a serving platter and keep warm in a low oven or cover with foil. Add the roasted peppers to the sauce in the skillet. Cook for 1 to 2 minutes, or until they're hot. Remove the bay leaves. Pour the sauce over the chicken and serve.

Excelsior Hotel, Rome, Italy

St. Andrew and the Beers of Belgium

WHEN it comes to drinking in Belgium . . . beer is the national choice, and the credit for spreading the brewer's skill throughout the nation goes to a Benedictine monk who was canonized as St. Andrew.

St. Andrew was trying to find out why wealthier citizens had a longer life expectancy, and eventually decided that drinking beer, in moderation, instead of water was the answer. And he was right. At the time, most water contained bacteria that could easily kill you. The heat in the beer brewing process killed much of that bacteria and made it safer to drink than water.

Today, Belgium produces over 600 different beers, and beer experts have chosen some of them as best of class worldwide. Two of their most unusual beers are *Kriek* and *Framboise*. *Kriek* has a cherry flavor and *Framboise* tastes like raspberries. The brewers say that organisms in the air around Brussels give these beers their special flavors and they can't be produced anywhere else.

The place in Brussels where I like to do my Belgian beer drinking is called Mort Subite, which means "sudden death." Years ago, the *Kriek* at Mort Subite had a high alcohol content but it tasted like cherry juice. A thirsty guy could easily drink two or three glasses, then try to stand up and fall to the floor—dead drunk. That is how the place got the name "sudden death." It is not an elegant café. It's old, noisy, smoky, and totally authentic. Life—before things became politically correct.

Chicken Braised in Beer with Belgian Endive

Makes 4 servings

About chicken. The chicken as we know it today is a descendant of the red jungle bird of Southeast Asia. It was domesticated in India as early as 2500 B.C.

Although chicken is inexpensive and plentiful today, it wasn't always so. From the late 1500s, when King Francis IV of France hoped for a "chicken in every pot," chicken was confined to Sunday dinner. The advent of modern poultry-raising technology in the twentieth century made chicken popular and available.

Fresh chicken is very perishable. For best results, buy and cook chicken the same day, especially if it is cut up or split. Nutritionally, chicken can be a very good source of lean protein. Light meat is lower in fat and calories than dark meat, and most of the fat and calories are in the skin. Take the skin off your chicken, even before you cook it, and you reduce the fat by more than half. Smaller broilers and fryers have less fat and calories than older birds such as roasters or stewing hens.

4 large Belgian endives, bottoms trimmed

2 tablespoons fresh lemon juice

Salt and freshly ground black pepper to taste

¼ cup vegetable oil

One 4-pound chicken, quartered

⅓ cup flour spread on a plate, seasoned with salt and pepper

2 tablespoons butter

4 teaspoons brown sugar

¼ cup minced onion

¼ cup water

½ cup dark ale or beer, preferably Belgian

1   Split the endives down the middle, lengthwise. Carefully cut out the hard white core in the center. Avoid cutting through to the bottom of the endives or they will fall apart. In a bowl, toss the endives with lemon juice and salt and pepper. Let them marinate while you brown the chicken.

2   In a heavy 5-quart casserole or Dutch oven over medium heat, heat the oil. While the oil is heating, dredge the chicken in flour and shake off any excess. Begin by adding the dark leg parts to the casserole and sauté, turning on occasion, for 5 to 7 minutes or until the skin is golden. Remove the pieces to a separate bowl and brown the remaining breast parts in the same way.

3   Discard the oil in the casserole, but keep the drippings. Add the butter and melt it over medium heat. When the butter is golden brown, add the endives and sprinkle the sugar over the

(continued)

91

halves. Sauté over medium-high heat, turning on occasion, for 2 to 3 minutes per side, or until the endives are golden brown and glistening. Add any remaining lemon juice the endives have marinated in, along with the minced onion and sauté, stirring, for another 3 to 4 minutes, or until they're softened.

4   Set the browned chicken leg parts over the endives, including any juices the chicken has given off in the bowl, and add the water and beer. In the saucepan, bring the liquid to a simmer and cook over very low heat for 20 minutes, turning the legs once. Add the breast parts, pressing the chicken into the endives as much as possible, cover, and continue to simmer gently for another 15 to 20 minutes, or until the chicken is tender and completely cooked through.

5   Remove the chicken and endives from the pot to a platter and cover with foil to keep warm as you finish the sauce. Boil the liquid down until 1 cup remains; season with salt and pepper to taste. Serve the chicken with endives and sauce spooned over the top.

Hotel Metropole, Brussels, Belgium

Chicken Cacciatore

1 TO PREPARE THE CHICKEN: Lightly season the chicken with salt and pepper, then dip it in the flour and shake off any excess.

2 TO COOK THE CHICKEN: In a deep casserole or a sauté pan that can accommodate all the chicken without crowding, heat the olive oil over medium heat. Cook the chicken, skin side down, for about 5 minutes, then turn and cook for 5 minutes more, or until the skin is golden. Remove the chicken to a plate, cover with foil, and set aside. Add the onion, bell pepper, carrot, and celery to the casserole and cook, stirring on occasion, for 5 minutes, or until the vegetables begin to soften. Add the mushrooms and cook, stirring, for 2 minutes longer, then add the garlic and cook for a few minutes, or until the mushrooms are tender.

3 Add the wine and cook for about 30 seconds, then add the red pepper flakes, if desired, the chicken stock, and tomatoes. Bring the liquid to a boil, scraping any of the browned bits which have stuck to the bottom of the pan. Return the chicken to the casserole and bring the liquid to a simmer, over moderate heat. Cook, partially covered, for about 30 minutes, or until the chicken is completely cooked through.

4 Remove the chicken to a plate and keep warm, lightly covered with foil. Boil the juices down to thicken the sauce, season with salt and pepper, then return the chicken to the sauce and warm for a minute. Serve the sauce over the chicken with rice, noodles, or boiled potatoes.

Mama Marie's Cucina, Las Vegas, Nevada

One 3- to 4-pound chicken, cut into 8 pieces; or 2 chicken breasts, split

Salt and freshly ground black pepper to taste

⅓ cup flour, spread on a plate

¼ cup olive oil

1 large yellow onion, thinly sliced

1 yellow or red bell pepper, seeded, cored, and thinly sliced

1 carrot, peeled and cut into thin disks

1 stalk celery, thinly sliced crosswise

8 to 10 ounces mushrooms, trimmed, wiped clean, and thinly sliced

1 large clove garlic, minced

¼ cup dry white wine or chicken stock

½ teaspoon dried red pepper flakes (optional)

½ cup chicken stock

1 cup chopped canned plum tomatoes

Cooked rice, noodles, or boiled potatoes for serving

The Legend of the Seas

THE *Legend of the Seas* is a cruise ship that was built in 1995 for the Royal Caribbean Cruise Line. It's 867 feet long, 105 feet wide, with 11 decks, and 902 cabins. It can maintain a speed of twenty-four knots.

The Knot

On land we measure speed in miles per hour or kilometers per hour. At sea it is measured in something called a "knot." Historians believe that sailors started using the knot during the 1400s. The technology was primitive. A piece of wood was tied to a rope. Every fifty feet there was a knot tied in the rope. They also had a sand-filled hourglass that measured twenty-eight seconds. They would throw the piece of wood over the side of the boat and when it hit the water, they would start the hourglass. When twenty-eight seconds of sand ran out, they counted the number of knots that had gone over the side, and that was the ship's speed.

Eventually the knot became standardized as the nautical mile, which is 6,080 feet—about 15 percent longer than a land mile. When sailors talk about a ship's speed, they just say "twenty knots," never "twenty knots per hour." Both the distance and the time measurement are included in the idea of a *knot*.

Chicken Breasts with Walnut Sauce

Makes 4 servings

About Walnuts. The walnut, a native of Persia, Europe, and North America, is second only to the almond in popularity and consumption. The major American species, the black walnut, is native to the Appalachians. The English walnut, which was brought to Europe by the Romans, is now grown mainly in California and is preferred by producers because it is easier to shell and not quite so bitter.

The Franciscan fathers brought walnut trees to the first missions in California. Today, the California walnut industry produces 95 percent of the walnuts eaten in the United States.

The walnut is an excellent food for vegetarians, because its protein is closer to animal protein than any vegetable other than the soybean.

4 chicken breast halves, bone in, skin on
Salt and freshly ground black pepper to taste
¼ cup flour
¼ cup olive oil
½ cup chopped onion
2 tablespoons balsamic vinegar
2 tablespoons port wine, Scotch whisky, Cognac, or fresh lemon juice
½ cup white wine
¾ cup chicken stock
⅓ cup heavy cream
1 teaspoon cornstarch
1 tablespoon water
¾ cup chopped walnuts

1 TO COOK THE CHICKEN: Preheat the oven to 400°F. Season the chicken with salt and pepper, and dip all sides of each breast in the flour. Shake off any excess flour.

2 In a large skillet, heat the olive oil. When the oil is hot, add the chicken, skin side down, and cook over medium-high heat for about 4 minutes on each side to brown. Transfer the chicken to a baking dish and bake for 20 to 25 minutes, or until cooked through.

3 TO MAKE THE SAUCE: Discard all but 2 tablespoons of the oil from the skillet in which the chicken was cooked. Heat this oil and sauté the onion over low heat for about 5 minutes, or until it's soft. When the onion is tender, add the vinegar, port, and white wine and boil the liquid down until only half remains. Add the chicken stock and heavy cream and bring to a simmer. Reduce the sauce to thicken it slightly.

4 Dissolve the cornstarch in the water and add it to the sauce. Bring the liquid to a boil and simmer over low heat for a minute. Season the sauce with salt and pepper and remove it from the heat. When the chicken is done, over low heat bring the sauce back to a simmer, but do not boil. Stir the walnuts into the sauce and spoon it over the chicken. Serve immediately.

Legend of the Seas, *Cruising Alaska*

The First Scots

*P*EOPLE have been living in Scotland for at least 6,000 years. The first inhabitants appear to have been groups of migrating hunters and fishermen. Next came the Celtic tribes who had been forced out of Europe. In 80 A.D., the Roman legions marched through, and finally the English.

The first references to Scotland's central city of Edinburgh were in the notes of Ptolemy, the ancient Roman writer who made his comments 160 A.D. The first site in the area to be colonized was probably a hill called Arthur's Seat.

Precisely which Arthur actually took a seat on Arthur's Seat isn't quite clear. Romantics like to point to the legendary King Arthur of the Round Table. But there is no evidence to support that view. There is, however, considerable evidence that this hill had at least four prehistoric forts and an ancient farming community.

Chicken Stovies with Clapshot

Makes 4 to 6 servings

1 TO BROWN THE CHICKEN: In a 6-quart Dutch oven or casserole over moderate heat, melt the butter. Add the onion and cook, uncovered, for 3 to 4 minutes, or until it's tender. Push the onion pieces to the edges of the pan and add the chicken, skin side down. Cook, turning frequently, for 3 to 4 minutes, or until the chicken has stiffened and is slightly colored. Cover and cook over very low heat, turning once, for about 10 minutes, or until the chicken is partially cooked. Remove the chicken to a plate and reserve for later.

2 TO MAKE THE SAUCE AND COOK THE CHICKEN: Stir the flour into the fat and onions and cook, stirring for a minute or two to cook out the raw flour taste. Add $1\frac{1}{2}$ cups of the broth and whisk as it comes to a boil. Simmer over low heat for 5 minutes, then add the cream, if using (if you don't add the cream, add $\frac{1}{2}$ cup more of the chicken broth). Return the dark meat (thighs and drumsticks) to the casserole, and simmer over moderate heat, uncovered, for 5 minutes. Turn the chicken over and add the breast meat and wings to the casserole. Cook on one side for 5 minutes, turn the chicken pieces over, and cook for another 5 minutes, or until the chicken is cooked through.

3 Preheat the oven to 475°F. Add the ham and parsley to the chicken and transfer it and the sauce to a 9-x-13-inch baking pan.

4 TO MAKE THE CLAPSHOT: In a 4-quart saucepan, in water to cover, boil the rutabaga cubes for 5 minutes. Add the turnips and potatoes and boil for 10 to 15 minutes longer, or until they're cooked through. Drain and toss with 1 tablespoon of butter and season with salt and black pepper. Top the chicken with this "clapshot," then sprinkle the fresh bread crumbs and melted butter onto the clapshot.

5 TO FINISH THE DISH: Put the chicken and clapshot in the oven and bake for 5 minutes, or until the bread crumbs are brown and the sauce is bubbly.

Gleneagles, Perthshire, Scotland

For the Sauce and the Chicken:

4 tablespoons unsalted butter

1 onion, cut into ¾-inch dice

1 whole frying chicken, cut into 8 pieces

3 tablespoons flour

1½ to 2 cups chicken broth

½ cup heavy cream (optional)

8 ounces baked or cooked smoked ham, cut into ½-inch dice

½ cup finely chopped fresh flat-leaf parsley

For the Clapshot:

1 pound rutabaga, peeled and cut into ¾-inch cubes

Two white turnips (½-pound), peeled and cut into ¾-inch cubes

4 small all-purpose potatoes (1 pound), peeled and cut into ¾-inch cubes

1 tablespoon butter plus 2 tablespoons melted butter

Salt and freshly ground black pepper to taste

1 cup coarsely made fresh bread crumbs (see Note)

NOTE: To make fresh bread crumbs, remove the crusts of a good quality white or sourdough bread and process the slices in a food processor until you have coarse fresh bread crumbs.

Chicken Carino

4 tablespoons vegetable oil

1½ pounds boneless, skinless chicken breast, cut into bite-sized pieces

Salt and freshly ground black pepper to taste

About 1 cup flour, on a flat plate

1 teaspoon minced garlic

3 tablespoons balsamic or red wine vinegar

½ cup chicken stock

3 cups bite-sized bell pepper pieces (a mixture of red, green, and yellow)

1 cup thinly sliced mushrooms

About vinegar. Vinegar has been around for 10,000 years. It is a 4 to 6 percent solution of acetic acid, produced from the action of bacteria on alcohol. The name comes from *vin aigre,* French for "sour wine."

Vinegar is often made from the distilled juice of fruits or rice. Their various flavors give different vinegars distinct characteristics.

Vinegar holds better if shielded from air, light, and cold. Vinegars are made from most wines, and in hundreds of flavorings. It is easy to make your own flavored vinegars by adding herbs to the bottles.

1 Preheat the oven to 375°F.

2 In a sauté pan large enough to hold all of the ingredients, heat the oil over medium heat.

3 Season the chicken pieces with the salt and pepper, then dredge them in the flour, shaking off any excess. Add them to the hot oil and cook the chicken on all sides until it's golden in color and fully cooked. Remove the cooked chicken to a strainer set over a bowl and let the oil drain off.

4 Pour any excess oil out of the pan, return the pan to the heat, and add the garlic. Cook, stirring for 1 minute. Slowly add the vinegar and cook for 30 seconds. Add the stock and bring to a boil. Add the peppers and mushrooms and cook, stirring from time to time, for 3 minutes. Place the chicken back into the pan.

5 Put the pan into the preheated oven for 5 minutes and serve.

Carino Ristorante, New York City

The Gastronomic Triumph of Napoleon

ABOUT twelve miles to the south of the Belgian city of Brussels is the town of Waterloo, which is thought of as the battlefield where the army of Napoleon was defeated by the Duke of Wellington. Actually, Waterloo was not the field of battle but the town from which Wellington sent the dispatch announcing his victory.

Wellington's troops were stationed to the north, defending Brussels. On the morning of June 18, 1815, Napoleon was ready for battle, but rain slowed everything down and he couldn't start his attack until 11 A.M. The assault on the English continued throughout the day, and by evening Wellington's reserves were used up. The Duke's only hope was nightfall or the arrival of his Prussian allies.

At 7:30 P.M., the Prussians under the command of General Blucher joined the battle. Blucher was not a dispassionate professional like Wellington. Napoleon had frustrated Germany's hopes for national unity and Blucher hated Napoleon. He saw this battle as a chance for revenge. The combined troops of Blucher and Wellington were too great for Napoleon, and within two hours the battle was over. The rain, the morning delay, and the few extra hours of light gave Wellington his victory.

Militarily Wellington won, but from a gastronomic viewpoint the outcome was completely different. The Duke's dish, Beef Wellington, has virtually disappeared from contemporary cooking, while the Emperor's Napoleon is still found in pastry shops throughout the world.

Chicken Waterzooi

4 tablespoons unsalted butter

2 medium onions, finely chopped

4 leeks, white parts only, thoroughly
washed and sliced into 3-inch-long
pieces

One 4-pound whole chicken, giblets and
fat removed from cavity

6 cups reduced-sodium chicken stock

⅛ teaspoon dried thyme, crushed

¼ teaspoon saffron

1 bay leaf

4 large carrots, peeled

4 stalks celery, washed

4 medium red new potatoes

½ teaspoon salt, plus more to taste

Freshly ground black pepper to taste

1 cup heavy cream

2 cups loosely packed fresh parsley leaves,
washed

Food lovers agree that some of the finest food in Europe is served in the homes and restaurants of Brussels. The major influences on the city's food come from the French and the Dutch, but you can also taste elements that came along during the years when Belgium was ruled by the Spanish and the Austrians.

Waterzooi is one of the most famous dishes. It's somewhere between a soup and a stew.

Note that while this recipe is easy, it does take some time to prepare. Ideally, you would make it a day ahead and finish the recipe on the day of serving.

1   In a 6-quart soup pot over low heat, melt the butter. Add the onions and leeks, cover, and stew gently for about 5 minutes, or until they are softened but not golden.

2   Place the chicken, breast side up, over the onions and leeks. Add the chicken stock, thyme, saffron, and bay leaf and enough water to cover the chicken by three quarters. Bring the liquid to a simmer, cover, and simmer for 20 minutes, turning the bird once, or until the chicken is partially cooked.

3   While the chicken is cooking, cut the carrots into 2-inch rounds. Cut the celery into 2-inch pieces. Peel and quarter the potatoes (keep them in cold water until needed so they do not discolor).

4   After the chicken has simmered for 20 minutes, add the carrots, celery, potatoes, ½ teaspoon salt, and pepper and simmer for another 25 minutes, or until the vegetables are very tender and the chicken is completely cooked through.

5   Remove the chicken from the pot to a platter and cool long enough so you can remove the skin without burning your fingers. As this is cooling, strain the broth into a large bowl, reserving the vegetables, and discard the bay leaf. Return the broth to the pot, skim off excess fat, and boil it down until 5 cups remain; season with salt and pepper.

6 When the chicken is cool enough to handle, remove and discard the skin. Remove as much of the cooked chicken as you can, in long thin strips. (Note: You can do the entire recipe up to this point a day in advance.) Mince the parsley.

7 When ready to serve, add the cream to the broth, along with the reserved vegetables and chicken strips. Simmer gently without boiling until the ingredients are reheated. Season with salt and pepper and stir in the parsley; serve immediately.

Hotel Metropole, Brussels, Belgium

The Food of Lombardia

*T*HE province of Lombardia, at the base of the Alpine mountain range, forms the center of Italy's northern border. Lombardia got its name from the Lombards, a German tribe that invaded Italy in the 500s. And invasion has been a serious problem for the area ever since.

During the 700s, Charlemagne came into the neighborhood and set himself up as king. Then Barbarossa arrived and sacked the place. In the 1500s, the French took over, followed by the Austrians, and the Spanish. Then came a second period of domination by the French under Napoleon, and finally a second period of domination by the Austrians. Lombardia didn't actually become part of Italy until 1859. A difficult history in terms of power and politics, but very tasty in terms of what each of the invaders brought to the Lombardian plate.

Today, Lombardia is the third-richest province in Europe, and Milan, its regional capital, is the country's financial center. Milan is well-known as a focus for banking, communications, fashion, and publishing. But it's also the heart of an important agricultural area, and the source of some of Italy's best cooking.

The Spanish arrived in the middle of the 1500s, and during their two hundred years of rule, they introduced rice-growing to northern Italy, along with the recipe which eventually became risotto. The Spanish also imported saffron. Together these two ingredients produce *risotto alla Milanese,* one of the most traditional dishes of the city. The Spanish also brought in *cassoela,* a dish of braised pork, sausages, and cabbage. The Milanese consider *cassoela* as one of their great comfort foods.

The Austrians took over from the Spanish in the early 1700s, and you can taste their influence in a dish like *costoletta Milanese,* a pounded and breaded veal chop with the bone in, sautéed in butter. Very similar to the schnitzel dishes of Austria and Germany.

Other classic recipes from Milan include *minestrone alla Milanese,* a vegetable soup that has become a favorite throughout Italy; *osso buco alla Milanese,* braised veal shank cooked with garlic, parsley, and lemon zest; *bollito misto,* a collection of boiled meats and one of the great winter dishes; and *polenta,* made from corn-meal, it is Italy's answer to grits. Polenta is served as a soft mush or dried and cut into blocks, and then sautéed.

The cows of Lombardia give excellent milk, which is used to make butter, which is in turn used for much of the cooking instead of oil. The local dairy farmers also produce a wide selection of cheeses; their most famous is a fresh Gorgonzola.

Burt Wolf

Taveggia Café, Milan, Italy. Home of the original Campari, and worth a stop just to taste the difference.

Chicken with Citrus Sauce

6 chicken breast halves, skin on, bone in

Salt and freshly ground black pepper
    to taste

2 sprigs fresh rosemary, chopped;
    or 1 teaspoon dried

3 small cloves garlic, peeled and thinly
    sliced

3 shallots, peeled and thinly sliced

4 tablespoons olive oil

½ cup pine nuts (2 ounces)

¼ cup dry white wine

1 tablespoon red wine vinegar

¼ cup fresh lemon juice

½ cup orange juice

⅔ cup chicken broth

½ cup golden raisins

About raisins. In 1873, a California grape grower had his entire crop scorched by hot sun. Instead of throwing out the dehydrated grapes, he brought them to a local grocer and convinced the grocer that the crop was raisinated grapes, a rare Persian delicacy. That was the beginning of the California raisin industry.

Raisins are grapes that have been dried to a point that prevents the development of enzymes that cause spoilage, which means they keep for a long time. To store raisins properly, remove them from the carton they come in, and place them in an airtight container in the refrigerator. To plump out raisins that have become too dry, soak them in water or fruit juice.

1   TO MARINATE THE CHICKEN: Rub the chicken with salt, pepper, rosemary, garlic, shallots, and 1 tablespoon of the olive oil and marinate it, in a glass or ceramic dish, in the refrigerator for 1 hour or longer. It tastes best if you marinate it overnight.

2   Preheat the oven to 350° F.

3   In a large casserole, heat the remaining 3 tablespoons of olive oil along with the marinade ingredients for 5 minutes, and sauté the chicken in the marinade, skin side down. Add the remaining ingredients. Simmer, uncovered, over medium heat for 3 to 4 minutes to concentrate the flavor and thicken the sauce.

4   Transfer the chicken to the oven and bake, uncovered, for 20 minutes, or until the chicken is cooked through. Remove the chicken to a platter and cover with foil to keep warm. Over high heat, boil the pan juices until thick. Season with salt and pepper. Serve the chicken with spoonfuls of sauce, nuts, and raisins over the top.

Four Seasons Hotel, Milan, Italy

Greek-Style Chicken

Makes 4 servings

About oregano. Oregano is a more highly flavored variety of marjoram; both are members of the mint family. Oregano grows as a compact bushy plant with tiny dark green leaves and purple and white blossoms. The greater part of the crop is harvested and marketed dried, but fresh oregano is always available.

1 Preheat the oven to 350°F.

2 In a pot of water, parboil the potatoes for 10 minutes, until only partially cooked through. Drain and pat them dry. Cut the halves lengthwise into thick fingers.

3 Sprinkle both sides of the chicken breast halves with the oregano and salt and pepper.

4 Using an ovenproof large sauté pan or wide Dutch oven, warm the oil over moderately high heat. Add the chicken breasts and sauté on one side until lightly browned, about 5 minutes. Turn the breasts and fit the potatoes into the empty areas of the pan. Cook for 5 minutes, turning to brown the potatoes on all sides.

5 Add the eggplant fingers and cook for 3 minutes. Nestle the garlic wheels in the bottom of the pan and cook for 2 minutes. Pour on half of the lemon juice and all the stock; bring to a boil.

6 Place the pan in the oven and bake for 15 minutes.

7 Divide the chicken, potatoes, eggplant, and garlic among 4 plates. Return the pan to moderately high heat and stir in the olives, parsley, and the remaining lemon juice. Cook, stirring, until heated through. Pour some of the sauce over each portion of chicken and serve.

Four Seasons Hotel, Toronto, Canada

2 large potatoes, peeled and halved lengthwise

4 boneless or bone-in, skinless chicken breast halves

¼ cup dried oregano, crushed

Salt and freshly ground black pepper to taste

¼ cup vegetable oil

1 large eggplant, peeled and cut into thick fingers

1 whole head of garlic, cut horizontally in half to make 2 "wheels"

Juice of 2 lemons

1 cup chicken stock

1 cup pitted and chopped black olives, or more to taste

¼ cup chopped fresh parsley

Chicken with Macadamia Nuts

1 pound boneless, skinless chicken breast
meat, cut into ½-inch dice

1 egg white

4 quarts salted water

2 cups peeled carrots, cut on the diagonal
into ½-inch pieces

2 cups trimmed peeled asparagus, cut on
the diagonal into ½-inch pieces

⅓ cup vegetable oil

1 tablespoon minced garlic

4 scallions, white and green parts, thinly
sliced

1 cup chopped macadamia nuts

3 tablespoons hoisin sauce

4 teaspoons cornstarch mixed with
3 tablespoons water

Salt to taste

About The Regent, Hong Kong. The Regent, is one of the world's great hotels and is presently run by Thomas Gurtner, one of the world's great hotel keepers. The property is located on the Kowloon waterfront overlooking Victoria Harbor. For over 30 years, The Regent restaurants have been famous for the quality of their food and service.

1 In a bowl, marinate the chicken in the egg white while you parboil the vegetables.

2 In a pot, bring the water to a boil and add the carrots. Cover and bring the water back to a boil and cook for a minute. Add the asparagus and boil for another minute. Drain the vegetables, cool them in cold water, and set aside.

3 In a wok or large skillet, heat the vegetable oil. When very hot, add the chicken and stir-fry over high heat for 1 minute, or until the chicken is opaque. Add the garlic, carrots, and asparagus and continue to stir-fry for 1 minute more to heat the vegetables through and finish cooking the chicken.

4 Add the scallions, macadamia nuts, and hoisin sauce and stir-fry for 30 seconds. Add the dissolved cornstarch and simmer for 30 seconds. Season with salt.

The Regent, Hong Kong

Hong Kong

*F*OR hundreds of years, Canton has been the capital city of southern China. It sits on the banks of the Pearl River, which empties out into the South China Sea. At the mouth of the river, about eighty miles from Canton, is the little island of Hong Kong. People have been living on Hong Kong for over 6,000 years, and until the middle of the 1800s it was a quiet place with a small population that made a living from the sea.

These days Hong Kong is one of the busiest and most modern cities in the world. And perhaps because it is physically so small—only seventeen square miles—it loves the idea of being big in every other way.

The Chinese words *Hong Kong* mean "Fragrant Harbor," which is a perfect description of the place. No matter what happens to it, it always comes up smelling like a rose. Hong Kong has also been described as being like a rubber ball—the harder you throw it, the higher it bounces. And it appears that at the heart of Hong Kong's ability to bounce back are two things: a population that can easily adapt to change and a government that supports business as the world changes.

The government believes that if someone wants to start a business he'll probably know enough about that business to make the venture a modest success. And it is the government's job to do everything it can to help the business become successful. The people running the government also believe that everybody is going to pay their taxes, and they believe that for two reasons. First of all, they feel that people are basically honest. And second, they feel that they've kept the taxes here in Hong Kong so low, that it costs more to cheat them than to pay them.

Because Hong Kong has been faced with an extraordinary level of change, it has mastered the techniques of transition. The key word is *flexibility*. They know when it's time to make a shift. If you have a small factory that is making typewriter keyboards and typewriters are no longer a growing business, but computers are, it's time to shift to computer keyboards. No problem. No rigidity. They'll make the change overnight.

Jerk Chicken with Mango Relish

⅛ teaspoon ground cloves

1 teaspoon paprika

1 teaspoon onion powder

1 teaspoon chili powder

½ teaspoon ground black pepper

1 teaspoon ground cinnamon

¾ teaspoon salt

3 tablespoons vegetable oil

1 clove garlic, minced

Six (6 to 8 ounce) boneless, skinless chicken cutlets, ½ inch thick

2 cups grapefruit juice

¼ cup brown sugar

2 cinnamon sticks

2 tablespoons red wine vinegar

¼ cup raisins

1 small onion, finely diced

1 red bell pepper, seeded and finely diced

1 green bell pepper, seeded and finely diced

2 mangoes, peeled and cut into ½-inch dice

Vegetable spray

1   In a glass or stainless mixing bowl, combine the cloves, paprika, onion powder, chili powder, black pepper, ground cinnamon, and salt. Add the vegetable oil and garlic and marinate the chicken cutlets in the mixture, covered, in the refrigerator while you make the relish.

2   In a small saucepot over medium heat, combine the grapefruit juice, brown sugar, cinnamon sticks, and vinegar. Simmer over medium heat until the volume is reduced by half and 1¼ cups remain. Add the raisins, onion, and peppers and simmer over low heat until most of the liquid has evaporated and the mixture begins to look shiny. Add the mangoes, stir for a few seconds, and remove from the heat and cool; you should have about 3 cups; discard the cinnamon sticks.

3   Spray a 10-inch skillet or stovetop grill pan with vegetable spray and set it over medium heat. Add the chicken breasts and cook for 3 to 6 minutes per side, or until they're completely cooked through. Remove them from the heat and cool for 2 minutes.

4   Slice the chicken on the diagonal into thin slices and fan them out on a plate. Surround each portion of chicken with about ½ cup of mango chutney.

Edgewater Beach Hotel, Naples, Florida

The Origins of Naples, Florida

*N*APLES, Florida, is one of the richest and fastest-growing cities in America. But because it sits on a strip of land that runs between the Gulf of Mexico and the fragile ecosystem of the Everglades, the residents are deeply involved in protecting their natural environment. In other words, Naples loves the good life but it is just as concerned with its wildlife.

In 1885, Walter Haldeman, the owner of the *Louisville Courier* newspaper, sailed down the west coast of Florida. He was looking for a healthy spot to build a winter home for his family. At the time, the lower west coast of Florida was almost totally deserted. There was no one in Naples—no houses, no tents, no Native Americans. There wasn't even a Naples, but there was a beautiful seven-mile crescent beach lined with pine trees and palm trees. Haldeman and a group of his friends bought the land and drew up the plans for Naples.

The world's last stand of Cypress, Corkscrew Sanctuary, Naples, Florida

Pecan-Crusted Chicken

4 large boneless, skinless chicken breast
  halves

8 teaspoons Dijon-style mustard

1 cup finely ground pecans (see Note)

1 cup fresh bread crumbs (see Note)

2 tablespoons vegetable oil

2 pounds sweet potatoes, peeled and cut
  into 1-inch dice

2 tablespoons butter

¾ cup plain low-fat yogurt

Salt and freshly ground black pepper
  to taste

½ cup finely diced banana

½ cup finely diced red bell pepper

½ cup finely diced yellow bell pepper

1 to 2 tablespoons minced jalapeño
  pepper

1 tablespoon chopped fresh cilantro

Juice of 1 lime

About pecans. The pecan, a member of the hickory nut family, is America's native nut, grown mainly in the southern states. George Washington planted pecan trees at Mount Vernon and is said to have carried pecan nuts in his pockets throughout the Revolutionary War. Thomas Jefferson grew pecans in his gardens at Monticello.

Pecans, like all nuts, are good sources of protein. The oil in pecans is high in polyunsaturates and the nut is very low in sodium.

You can buy pecans in the shell, shelled in halves, and shelled crushed. Shelled pecan nuts can be ground in a food blender or smashed with a rolling pin. Shelled, especially ground pecans, are very perishable. They keep best tightly covered in the refrigerator or freezer.

1 TO COOK THE CHICKEN: Preheat the oven to 375° F. Brush each side of the chicken with 1 teaspoon of mustard. In a bowl, combine the pecans and bread crumbs and press this mixture onto both sides of the chicken. In a 10-inch skillet, heat the vegetable oil and sauté the chicken for 1 minute on each side. Transfer the chicken to a baking pan and bake for 30 minutes, or until it's cooked through.

2 TO MAKE THE SWEET POTATO PUREE: While the chicken is cooking, in a pot of water to cover, boil the sweet potatoes for about 20 minutes, or until they're tender. Drain the sweet potatoes and mash them together with the butter and yogurt. Season with salt and pepper.

3 TO MAKE THE SALSA: In a bowl, combine the banana with the peppers, cilantro, lime juice, and salt and pepper.

4 TO SERVE THE CHICKEN: Mound the sweet potatoes in the center of each plate, place the chicken on the potatoes, and garnish with the salsa.

Boca Raton Resort and Club, Florida

NOTE: To grind the nuts, put them in a food processor and pulse them until finely ground; do not overdo this step or the nuts will turn oily and pasty.

NOTE: To make the bread crumbs, tear 4 slices of packaged white bread and pulse them in a food processor until crumbed.

Who Put the Palm in Palm Beach?

$\mathcal{P}$ARIS Singer was one of the seventeen illegitimate children of Isaac Singer, the founder of the Singer Sewing Machine Company. He was also a member of the Palm Beach crowd. Paris had a pal named Addison Mizner who was living in New York and in bad health. Singer convinced Mizner that he could regain his health by moving to Palm Beach.

Mizner had come from a prominent California pioneering family. His father had been a U.S. ambassador to South America, and he grew up living the good life. He had been a decorator who worked with successful architects, a real estate developer, a painter, a collector of rare antiques, a successful gold miner, and a boxer.

He showed up in Palm Beach just as one of Florida's land booms was getting underway, and he soon became a popular architectural decorator. Singer and Mizner lived it up in Palm Beach while building it up for Mizner's clients.

Mizner was actually not the perfect architect. It appears that his memory for detail was sometimes impaired and he could forget little things—like the kitchen in a huge mansion. What can I tell you? Mizner had a lot on his mind. In 1925, he decided to build the Cloister Inn.

Today, it is known as the Boca Raton Resort and Club. The Mizner style is all over the place. He loved Spanish architecture, gardens, Moorish fountains, and antique furniture.

Grilled Chicken with Sweet Potato Sauce

2 tablespoons vegetable oil

½ cup finely chopped celery

½ cup finely chopped onion

¼ teaspoon ground cinnamon

⅛ teaspoon ground mace

⅛ cup honey

2 cups chopped peeled sweet potato

1 cup apple cider

2½ cups chicken stock

Salt and freshly ground black pepper
    to taste

2 chicken breasts, skinned, boned,
    and split

½ cup chopped pecans

1 tablespoon chopped fresh parsley

½ cup diced red bell pepper

1   In a saucepan over medium heat, heat the oil. Add the celery and onion and sauté for 3 to 4 minutes, stirring, until softened.

2   Add the cinnamon and mace and stir to distribute. Stir in the honey and sweet potato. Add the cider and chicken stock. Bring to a boil over high heat, then lower to medium heat and cook for 30 minutes.

3   Puree the mixture in a food processor. Taste and adjust the seasoning with salt and pepper. If the sauce is too thin, place in a saucepan and cook it down over medium heat until the sauce is the desired consistency. If the sauce is too thick, add more chicken stock and heat through. Set the sauce aside.

4   Preheat the oven to 375° F. Preheat a stovetop grill or ridged frying pan.

5   Season the chicken breasts with salt and pepper. When the grill or frying pan is very hot, grill the chicken breasts for 3 minutes on each side. Then, remove them to a baking pan and place them in the oven for 10 minutes, or until they're fully cooked. (If the breasts are thin enough, they can be cooked entirely on the grill, about 5 minutes on each side. A charcoal grill or regular cast-iron skillet may also be used.)

6   To serve, pour some sauce on each of 4 plates and sprinkle with pecans, parsley, and red bell pepper. Place the cooked chicken over the sauce.

1789 Restaurant, Washington, D.C.

MEAT

Bahamian Lamb Curry

Beef Stewed in Beer

Beef with Dill Sauce and Horseradish Crust

Cola Baked Ham

Crispy Fillet of Lamb with Peanut Butter Sauce

Devil's Mess

Devil's Mess Omelet

Fig-Glazed Pork Chops

Filet Mignon Madeira

Highland Meatballs with Mustard and Whisky Sauce

Ginger Beef with Vegetables

Seared Southwestern Bacon-Wrapped Beef Tenderloin

Nut-Crusted Pork Tenderloin

Honey-Glazed Pork with Garlic Mashed Potatoes

A Brief Introduction to the Bahamas

*T*HE most northerly island in the Bahamas lies about a hundred and fifty miles off the east coast of Florida, at about the same latitude as Palm Beach. There are over seven hundred islands in the Bahama chain, and they swing down to the southeast until they come to an end just above the Dominican Republic.

When Christopher Columbus finally hit land in the New World, it was on one of the tiny islands of the Bahamas. Spanish explorers following Columbus called the area *Baja Mar,* which means "the shallow sea." Eventually, the islands came to be known as the Bahamas.

The first people to live in the area were known as the Lucayans, which means "people of the islands." By all accounts, they were a friendly group. They had started out about two thousand years ago in South America and moved north through the Caribbean. One of the reasons they kept moving was to avoid another tribe known as the Caribs. The Caribs, like many modern nutritionists, believed that the more different foods you included in your diet the healthier you would be. The Caribs included the *Lucayans* in their diet. And that's one of the reasons the word *cannibal* is found in the languages of Europe. Unfortunately, when the Spanish showed up, things did not get better. The Lucayans got out of the food chain only to find themselves in the chains of slavery. Within twenty-five years they all died and the islands were deserted.

Bahamian Lamb Curry

About curry. The term *curry* describes a blend of spices commonly used in Indian cooking. In India, curry is usually not bought, but blended at home from curry leaves, garlic, ginger, pepper, yellow turmeric, and other spices. Because of the freedom in the amounts and types of spices used, there is no standard definition of what makes up a curry seasoning.

1   In a saucepan large enough to hold the lamb in a single layer (or in batches), heat the oil over moderate heat. Pat the lamb cubes dry with paper towels and brown them, over medium-high heat, for about 10 minutes, until brown on all sides. As each batch is done, remove them to a bowl.

2   When the lamb is brown, discard the fat from the saucepan and replace it with the butter. Melt the butter over moderate heat, then add the onions and celery and cook, uncovered, stirring once or twice, for about 5 minutes, or until they're tender. Add the garlic, curry powder, and cumin and sauté for about a minute to cook the spices.

3   Add the tomato paste to the curry, then whisk in the chicken broth, thyme, and bay leaf. Return the lamb to the saucepan and add the carrots and potatoes; season with ½ teaspoon of salt. Bring the liquid to a boil over high heat, cover, and simmer over low heat, with the lid ajar, for 1 to 1¼ hours, or until the lamb and the vegetables are tender.

4   Strain the solids, and thoroughly degrease the juices. Discard the bay leaf and return the degreased juices to the saucepan. Over high heat, boil the juices down until 1 cup remains. Add the coconut milk, return the meat and vegetable solids to the pot, and simmer the stew to reheat. Stir in the lime juice and season with salt and pepper. Serve over plain boiled rice and garnish with cilantro, if desired.

Atlantis, Paradise Island, Bahamas

¼ cup vegetable oil

2 pounds boneless lamb shoulder (see Note) or beef chuck, trimmed of fat and cut into 1-inch cubes

2 tablespoons butter

1 cup finely diced onions

½ cup finely chopped celery

3 cloves garlic, minced

3 tablespoons curry powder

½ teaspoon ground cumin

1 tablespoon tomato paste

4 cups chicken broth

¼ teaspoon dried thyme

1 bay leaf

4 medium carrots, peeled and cut into ½-inch dice

1½ pounds all-purpose potatoes, peeled and cut into ½-inch dice

½ teaspoon salt, plus extra to taste

¾ cup coconut milk, regular or light

2 tablespoons fresh lime juice

Freshly ground black pepper to taste

¼ cup chopped fresh cilantro for garnish (optional)

Cooked rice for serving

NOTE: If you can't find boneless lamb shoulder, buy 3 to 3¼ pounds of lamb shoulder chops. When you get them home, cut out the bones and remove as much of the fat as possible. Cube the remaining meat into 1-inch dice.

The Hotel Metropole, Brussels

T HE Hotel Metropole opened in 1895 and was designed to express the great luxury that was available in Brussels at the end of the nineteenth century.

The entrance hall is a French renaissance foyer in marble with vaulted ceilings, crystal chandeliers, and Oriental rugs. The reception area looks as it did over one hundred years ago: polished woods, brass trimming, uniformed attendants. Beneath the Corinthian columns of the bar are palm trees—a reminder of Belgium's expansion into Africa.

There's an outside terrace and a café that were already famous in the 1800s. Contemporary interior designers often feel that less is more, but the Belle Époque boys who built these rooms clearly believed that more is more.

The hotel also has a Michelin-rated restaurant where the chef prepares some of the traditional foods of Brussels.

Beef Stewed in Beer

Makes 4 to 6 servings

One of the traditional dishes in the Flemish districts of Belgium is Beef Stewed in Beer. Cubes of beef are browned with onions, stewed in a rich Belgian beer, then flavored with a touch of red currant jelly and red wine vinegar. The jelly and vinegar give the dish a sweet and sour edge. It's served with boiled potatoes, applesauce, and . . . more rich Belgian beer.

1 Season the flour with salt and pepper. Toss the beef cubes evenly with the mixture, shaking off any excess, and set aside for later.

2 In a 4- to 5-quart heavy casserole or Dutch oven over medium heat, heat the oil until hot (when the beef hits the oil, the fat should sizzle). In 2 batches so as to not crowd the pan, brown the beef on all sides until it's a deep golden color, and remove to a bowl.

3 Add the butter to the oil and melt, then add the onions and cook over medium high heat, stirring frequently, for about 15 minutes, or until the onions are soft and brown.

4 Slowly add the beer and stock to the onions, scraping the bottom of the pan with a wooden spoon to lift up the drippings. Set the meat over the onions and add the bay leaf and thyme, and season with salt and pepper. Bring the liquid to a simmer, cover, and cook over very low heat for 1½ hours, or until the beef is tender.

5 Uncover the pot and boil the liquid down a bit to thicken. Stir in the jelly or sugar and the vinegar and simmer for another minute. Remove the bay leaf and adjust the seasoning; serve immediately garnished with parsley.

Hotel Metropole, Brussels, Belgium

3 tablespoons flour

Salt and freshly ground black pepper to taste

2 pounds boneless beef chuck, cut into 2-inch cubes

¼ cup vegetable oil

2 tablespoons butter

8 medium onions, thinly sliced

12 ounces (¾ cup) dark beer or ale, preferably Belgian or stout

¼ cup beef stock

1 bay leaf

¼ teaspoon dried thyme, crushed

2 teaspoons red currant jelly or brown sugar

2 teaspoons red wine vinegar

¼ cup minced fresh parsley for garnish

The Traditional Foods of Bavaria

*B*AVARIAN specialties include *Leberkäse* which means liver-cheese . . . strange, since *Leberkäse* doesn't contain any liver or any cheese. It's actually a form of meat loaf that tastes like bologna. *Wurstteller* is a plate of five or six different sausages served with sauerkraut and potatoes. *Schweinebraten mit Blaukraut und Knödel* is roast pork with red cabbage and dumplings. Pork's knuckle, *Schweinshax'n,* is crispy, tasty, and very traditional for Bavaria. Mushrooms in cream sauce served over a giant dumpling is called *Pilzen mit Semmelknödel.* There's also a homemade pasta with melted cheese and onion called *Käsespätzle,* and for dessert—pancakes with almonds, raisins, and applesauce called *Kaiserschmarrn.* Big food for big appetites, and all of it worth the calories.

Two-fisted tourist, Munich, Germany

Beef with Dill Sauce and Horseradish Crust

Makes 4 servings

1 Tie a piece of string around the middle of each filet to keep it secure while cooking.

2 TO MAKE THE CRUST: In a small skillet over medium heat, heat the butter until golden, add the dried bread crumbs, and toss until well combined and immediately remove from the heat. Transfer the bread crumbs to a bowl, combine them with the horseradish, and season with salt. Set aside for later.

3 TO MAKE THE SAUCE: In a 9-inch skillet over medium heat, heat the butter. When melted, add the onion and sauté, stirring on occasion, for 3 to 4 minutes, or until the onion is tender and golden. Add the beef stock and simmer until ¾ cup remains. Add the cream and boil until you have 1 cup of liquid in total. Season with salt and pepper and remove from the heat.

4 TO COOK THE BEEF: Preheat the broiler or the oven to 475° F. Bring the salted water to a boil and add the filet mignons. Simmer them gently for about 5 minutes for rare, 7 minutes for medium-rare, and 10 minutes for medium-well done. (The simmering actually cooks the beef while keeping it tender.) Remove the filets with a slotted spoon and pat dry with paper towels. Set them on a broiler rack or baking sheet and top each filet with the horseradish crust.

5 Meanwhile, over low heat, bring the sauce back to a simmer, without boiling. Broil the beef just long enough to give the crust a golden hue, or bake for a few minutes, until the tops look a little dried out. Remove from the heat and set a filet mignon in the middle of a dinner plate and remove the string. Add the dill to the sauce and remove from the heat. Spoon some sauce over and around each filet and serve immediately.

Hotel Rafael, Munich, Germany

Four 6- to 8-ounce filet mignons, about 1½ inches thick

2 quarts salted water

For the Horseradish Crust:

2 tablespoons unsalted butter

¼ cup dried bread crumbs

3 tablespoons white prepared horseradish

Salt to taste

For the Sauce:

1 tablespoon unsalted butter

¼ cup minced onion

2 cups beef stock, fresh or, if canned, reduced sodium

¾ cup heavy cream

Salt and freshly ground black pepper to taste

½ cup minced fresh dill

Cola Baked Ham

One 10-pound ham (not cured or aged)

4 to 8 cups cola, depending on size of roasting pan

1 cup brown sugar

1 cup bread crumbs

2 teaspoons dry mustard

1 teaspoon freshly ground black pepper

1 Preheat the oven to 350° F. Remove the skin from the ham. Place the ham, fat side down, in a roasting pan. Add about 1 inch of cola to the pan. Bake for about 2½ hours, allowing 15 minutes per pound. Baste the ham frequently with the cola. Add more cola to the roasting pan during cooking to prevent burning. Turn the ham fat side up after 2 hours.

2 In a medium bowl, combine the brown sugar, bread crumbs, mustard, and pepper. After the ham has cooked a total of 2½ hours, remove the ham from the oven. Press the crumb coating onto the ham. Return to the oven for 30 to 40 minutes more, until the coating is golden and the ham is fully cooked.

American Festival Cafe, New York City

Crispy Fillet of Lamb with Peanut Butter Sauce

Makes 4 servings

1   TO PREPARE THE LAMB: Have the butcher remove the bone from the loin. With a sharp knife, remove the outside fat and tie a piece of string around the middle of each boneless loin chop so the filet section of the loin will not fall apart when you are cooking it.

2   On a flat plate, season the flour with salt and pepper. Dip all sides of the lamb in the seasoned flour and shake off any excess. In a medium non-stick skillet over high heat, heat the oil. When very hot, sear the lamb on all sides until it begins to get golden. Turn the heat to medium-low and cook for 5 to 10 minutes per side, depending on the thickness of the meat and the degree of doneness you prefer.

3   TO MAKE THE SAUCE: In a wide 10-inch skillet over medium heat, simmer the orange juice, chicken broth, and red pepper flakes for about 5 minutes or until only ¾ cup remains. Whisk in the peanut butter and season with salt and pepper.

4   TO SERVE: Remove the cooked lamb to a carving board and carefully remove the string. With tongs, center each piece on a dinner plate and spoon some of the sauce around the lamb. Serve immediately.

The Ritz-Carlton, Naples, Florida

4 loin lamb chops, about 1 inch thick, each weighing 8 ounces (Have the butcher remove the bone from the loin.)

2 tablespoons flour

Salt and freshly ground black pepper to taste

1 tablespoon vegetable oil

1 cup orange juice

1 cup chicken broth

¼ teaspoon red pepper flakes

¼ cup unhomogenized peanut butter

Devil's Mess

4 tablespoons vegetable oil

1 small onion, finely chopped

1 green bell pepper, seeded and finely sliced

1 pound hot Italian sausage, pressed out of their casings

2 small cloves garlic, minced

1 tablespoon ground cumin

2 teaspoons curry powder

¼ to ½ teaspoon cayenne

¼ teaspoon ground cardamom

1 cup dry red wine

¼ cup Worcestershire sauce

2 cups water

Salt to taste

1. In a 12-inch skillet over medium heat, heat the oil. Add the onion and pepper and cook, stirring on occasion, for 5 minutes, or until they're almost tender. Add the sausage, and sauté, uncovered, for 5 minutes, stirring continuously to crumble the mixture. Add the garlic, cumin, curry powder, cayenne, and cardamom and cook for a couple of minutes longer.

2. Add the wine and boil down for about 3 minutes or until half remains. Add the Worcestershire sauce and water and simmer for 30 minutes, or until about ½ cup of liquid remains in the bottom of the pan. Remove from the heat and season with salt.

Millie's Diner, Richmond, Virginia

Devil's Mess Omelet

Makes 2 servings

1 Preheat the broiler. In a 12-inch ovenproof skillet over medium heat, heat the butter. Add the Devil's Mess and cook for a minute to heat up the mixture.

2 Add the eggs to the pan and scramble them loosely. When the eggs are almost set, remove the skillet from the heat and sprinkle the cheese over the eggs. Transfer the skillet to the broiler and heat until the cheese is hot and melted, about 30 seconds.

3 Serve from the skillet; top each portion with 3 avocado slices.

2 tablespoons butter

1 cup Devil's Mess

6 eggs, lightly beaten

2 cups shredded sharp Cheddar cheese

6 slices avocado

Fig-Glazed Pork Chops

Four ¾-inch-thick pork chops

Salt and freshly ground black pepper
   to taste

1 cup fig preserves

1   Preheat the oven to 375° F. Season the chops with salt and pepper. Coat the chops with the fig preserves and bake for 30 minutes, uncovered, until fully cooked.

Virginia Beach, Virginia

Virginia Beach, Virginia

Filet Mignon Madeira

About Filet Mignon. Filet Mignon is a cut of meat about the size of a hockey puck. It is taken from the small end of a fillet of beef. Improperly cooked, it will also taste like a hockey puck.

1 TO MAKE THE SAUCE: In a 2-quart saucepan over medium heat, combine the Madeira, brown stock, ¼ cup chives or scallions, bay leaf, black pepper, and thyme. Simmer for about 30 minutes, or until the liquid has evaporated and only ¾ cup remains. Strain out the solids and reserve the liquid for later.

2 TO COOK THE FILET MIGNONS: Preheat the oven to 400° F. Brush a large ovenproof iron skillet (which will accommodate the filet mignons in a single layer, without crowding) with the oil and over high heat, heat until hot. Add the filets and sear for about 2 minutes per side. Transfer the skillet to the oven and cook for 8 to 10 minutes for rare. Cook for an additional 2 minutes for medium rare, or keep cooking until you reach the desired degree of doneness.

3 Very carefully remove the skillet from the oven and transfer the beef to a carving board. Holding the handle of the skillet with pot holders (it is still very hot from the oven), add the sauce and bring it to a boil with the cream; simmer for a minute. Remove the sauce from the heat and season with salt and pepper.

4 TO SERVE THE FILETS: Slice the beef into ¼-inch slices and center them on dinner plates. Spoon the sauce around and over the meat and garnish the sauce with chives or parsley.

Fiore's, Las Vegas, Nevada

1 cup Madeira wine

2 cups brown stock, preferably unsalted (This is usually available in a butcher or gourmet shop in the refrigerator case. If you cannot get brown stock, use unsalted beef stock.)

¼ cup minced fresh chives or scallions

1 bay leaf

½ teaspoon coarsely cracked black pepper

¼ teaspoon dried thyme, crushed

1 tablespoon vegetable oil

Six 6- to 8-ounce boneless filet mignons, 1½ inches thick

½ cup heavy cream

Salt and freshly ground black pepper to taste

3 tablespoons minced fresh chives or parsley for garnish

Highland Meatballs with Mustard and Whisky Sauce

4 slices packaged white bread, crusts
    removed, crumbled

½ cup milk for soaking

1 large egg

¾ teaspoon dried thyme

¾ teaspoon dried rosemary

½ teaspoon ground coriander

½ cup finely diced onion cooked in
    1 tablespoon oil until soft

1¾ pounds ground beef chuck, chicken,
    or turkey (see Note)

Salt and freshly ground black pepper
    to taste

⅓ cup dry bread crumbs for coating

4 tablespoons vegetable oil

5 tablespoons unsalted butter

¼ cup minced shallots

1 clove garlic, minced

20 ounces white mushrooms, stems
    removed, cut into ½-inch pieces

¼ cup Scotch whisky

¼ cup coarse-grain mustard

2 tablespoons flour

2¼ cups beef broth

1 bay leaf

6 medium carrots, peeled and cut into
    ¾-inch rounds

2 teaspoons sugar

3 leeks (½ pound), white parts only, cut
    into ¾-inch rounds

3 stalks celery (6 ounces), peeled and cut
    into ¾-inch lengths

NOTE: If you substitute ground turkey or
chicken, then season the poultry mix with
thyme and sage and omit the coriander.

When most people think about Scottish food they come up with shall we say, less than the most enticing images. First to mind is usually *Haggis,* a nationally famous dish made from the innards of sheep that have been chopped up and boiled in the lining of a sheep's stomach. And then they stop thinking about Scottish food and desperately try to think about something else. Reflect for a moment. You've undoubtedly heard people say: "Let's go out for French food, or Italian food, or Chinese food." But I'll bet you have never heard anybody say: "Let's go out for Scottish." And yet, for the last few years, I have been having really *good* meals in Scotland.

1 TO MAKE THE MEATBALLS: Soak the crumbled bread in the milk for 15 minutes, or until the bread is softened. Squeeze out the excess moisture and transfer the soaked bread to a food processor along with the egg, thyme, rosemary, and coriander. Process until combined, then add the cooked onions, two thirds of the meat, and salt and pepper. Process until blended. Transfer the mixture to a bowl, add the remaining meat, and mix with your hands. Roll the meat into thirty-two 1½-inch meatballs, then roll the meatballs in the dry bread crumbs, coating all sides.

2 TO COOK THE MEATBALLS AND MAKE THE SAUCE: In a 6- to 7-quart casserole over moderate heat, heat the vegetable oil and 2 tablespoons of the butter. In 2 batches, brown the meatballs, making sure they are crisp on all sides. When they are brown, remove them with a slotted spoon to a plate. Add the shallots to the remaining fat in the casserole and sauté for a couple of minutes, or until they're tender. Add the garlic and mushrooms and sauté for 2 to 3 minutes, or until they're tender. Add the whisky and boil, scraping up the juices on the bottom of the casserole into the whisky, and simmer for a minute or so or until the whisky has almost evaporated. Add the mustard and the flour and cook for a minute. Add 2 cups of the beef broth and bring it to a simmer, whisking all the while.

Add the bay leaf and simmer for a couple of minutes. Adjust the seasoning and return the meatballs to the sauce (the dish can be made a day or two in advance up to this point). Simmer the meatballs, uncovered, to heat them and finish cooking them while you make the vegetable garnish.

3   TO MAKE THE VEGETABLE GARNISH: In a separate 12-inch skillet over moderate heat, heat 2 tablespoons of the remaining butter. Add the carrots, sugar, and the remaining ¼ cup of beef broth. Cover and simmer for 3 to 4 minutes, or until the carrots are partially cooked. Add the leeks, celery, and parsnips and the water. Cover and simmer for 10 minutes longer, or until the vegetables are tender. Uncover the skillet, evaporate the liquid over high heat until the vegetables are glazed. Add the remaining tablespoon of butter and season with salt and pepper.

4   TO SERVE THE DISH: Discard the bay leaf. Spoon the meatballs onto a plate and top with mushrooms and gravy. Scatter glazed vegetables over the meatballs and garnish with the parsley. Serve with boiled potatoes or rice.

Gleneagles, Perthshire, Scotland

3 parsnips (½ pound), peeled and cut into ¾-inch lengths
¾ cup water
⅓ cup minced fresh parsley for garnish
Boiled potatoes or cooked rice for serving

Dim Sum in Hong Kong

*D*IM *sum* translates as "a point on the heart" or "touching the heart." And what does the touching is a collection of small foods designed to be taken with tea.

The best way to experience this tradition is to visit a restaurant that specializes in *dim sum*. This is the Ocean City restaurant in the New World Center, and it is one of the world's great presenters of *dim sum*. A *dim sum* restaurant should be huge, well lit, packed with eaters, noisy, and somewhat chaotic. Carts carrying steam baskets and dishes of food are wheeled around the tables by women. Each basket or dish contains a particular food. As they move through the restaurant, they describe the food on their trolley. The diners yell for what they want, and the servers serve. Each dish has a specific price, and each table has a card. Your card is stamped for each dish that you take. At the end of the meal, the waiter adds up the stamps and you find out what your meal cost. You can eat as much or as little as you like. But if you want to eat *dim sum* at its best, it's important to get to the restaurant early. If the place opens at noon, try and be there about fifteen minutes before. The food will be at its point of perfection and you will get a table for the first round of service. The later you come in, the more limited the selection. *Dim sum* is at its *most* magnificent on Sunday morning, when it is a traditional family meal . . . a gastronomic bedlam, and lots of fun.

Burt Wolf

Devoted dim sum *eater, Hong Kong*

Ginger Beef with Vegetables

About ginger. Fresh ginger is the root of the *Zingiber officinale* plant that is native to the United States, Asia, and China. Most of the ginger we get in the United States is grown in Jamaica and the West Indies. Ginger beer, a nonalcoholic drink made with grated fresh ginger, is popular throughout the Caribbean.

Good-quality fresh ginger is generally available and gives more flavor than the ground variety, though ground is usually preferred in baking. When buying fresh ginger, look for roots that are firm, not shriveled—the roots look like the finger and palm of your hand. Fresh ginger can be stored tightly wrapped for a few days in the refrigerator. Peeled and submerged in a jar of sherry wine, fresh ginger will last for up to six months. In cooking, slice the ginger very thinly or grate it.

Candied or crystallized ginger has been cooked and preserved in sugar syrup. It is best to use candied ginger in making desserts, but in a pinch, it can be washed of its sugar coating and used like regular fresh ginger.

2 cups water

1 cup celery, cut into 2½-x-¼-inch julienne

1 cup julienned carrots

3 tablespoons vegetable oil

1 tablespoon sesame oil

12 ounces flank steak, sliced against the grain, on an angle, cut into 4-x-½-inch strips

2 tablespoons minced fresh ginger

1 tablespoon minced garlic

1 teaspoon cornstarch dissolved in 1 tablespoon water

Salt to taste

1   In a wok or large skillet, bring the water to a boil. Add the celery and carrots and boil for a minute. Drain and discard the water and wipe the wok clean.

2   In the wok, heat the vegetable and sesame oils and stir-fry the beef for 1 minute. Add the ginger and garlic and stir-fry for 30 seconds. Add the parboiled celery and carrots and stir-fry for 30 seconds. Add the dissolved cornstarch and cook for a minute, or until the sauce begins to thicken. Season with salt and serve.

The Regent, Hong Kong

Virginia Beach

ON the twenty-sixth of April, 1607, 105 employees of the London Company arrived on the coast of what eventually became the city of Virginia Beach. They explored the area for four days, then moved inland and started the settlement at Jamestown.

The early settlers in Virginia took up residence along the James River, at the mouth of the Chesapeake Bay. These days it's where you will find the city of Virginia Beach. For nearly four hundred years, the people of the Virginia Beach area have been surrounded by a great variety of seafood—oysters, sturgeon, lobster, crabs, shrimp. During the 1600s, Captain John Smith wrote home to England that he had seen so many sea bass in the Chesapeake Bay that he thought he could walk across their backs without getting wet.

Virginia also became famous for its pork. Pigs can be raised without much supervision. The early Virginia colonists would fence their pigs *out,* not in. The pigs lived on whatever the settlers discarded and what they could find in the woods. When Virginia planters began developing a peanut crop, they used it as a cheap food source for the pigs. The pigs took on a peanut flavor. The most famous pigs from Virginia came from an area called Smithfield. They became so popular in the United States and in Europe that Queen Victoria of England had a standing order for six Smithfield hams every week.

The great planters of Virginia lived on huge estates which kept them rather isolated from the rest of the world. And it is in that sense of separation that we find the origins of southern hospitality. When somebody finally did show up, you wanted to keep them around as long as possible and have them tell you what was going on in the rest of the world. George Washington actually had two servants stationed at a crossroads with instructions to stop any interesting travelers and bring them home for dinner.

Seared Southwestern Bacon-Wrapped Beef Tenderloin

Makes 4 servings

About cumin. Cumin is a tall, feathery plant that is a member of the carrot family. The part used as a seasoning is the seeds, which are harvested, dried, roasted, and ground.

The Romans used cumin as a seasoning in their food and it remained popular throughout the Middle Ages. The biblical Hebrews believed cumin had the power to keep lovers from being fickle.

1 Preheat the oven to 450° F. Wrap the bacon around the outside of the circumference of the tenderloins and secure with toothpicks.

2 In a bowl, combine the seasonings and mix well. Brush the tenderloins with some of the oil and pat the seasoning mixture onto both sides.

3 Rub some oil into one or two 9-inch cast-iron pans and set them over high heat (open a window or put on the exhaust fan because this creates a lot of smoke).

4 Sauté the tenderloins for 2 minutes on each side and transfer them to a baking pan. Set them in the oven to finish cooking (about 10 minutes for rare, 12 minutes for medium-rare, and 14 minutes for medium depending on the thickness).

5 To present each portion, ladle some chili salsa on the bottom of the plate and set 3 triangles of toasted tortillas around the outside of the plate. Set a black bean cake on each of the toasted tortilla triangles, and set the cooked tenderloin in the center of the plate. Sprinkle with queso blanco or feta, and cilantro.

The Lucky Star, Virginia Beach

6 thick pieces bacon

Four 8-ounce beef tenderloins, 1½ inches thick

1 tablespoon ground cumin

1 tablespoon chili powder

½ teaspoon cayenne

1½ teaspoons paprika

¼ teaspoon dried thyme

¼ teaspoon freshly ground black pepper

¼ teaspoon ground cinnamon

1 tablespoon kosher salt

2 tablespoons vegetable oil

Red Chili Salsa (page 42)

12 triangles of tortillas, toasted

12 small Black Bean Cakes (page 162)

Crumbled queso blanco or feta cheese

Chopped fresh cilantro for garnish

The Story of Sunbathing

IN societies where the majority of the population was light-skinned, it was traditionally fashionable to do everything you could to avoid getting a suntan. Only common laborers who were forced to work outside, like farm workers or television reporters, ended up with a suntan. And if a woman had a suntan, it was a clear indication that she was from a lower station in life. When women of society went out, they did everything they could to avoid getting a suntan.

During the 1920s, however, things began to change. Lots of people were getting rich and looking for new and fashionable places to spend their money. The yachting crowd arrived, and what was the point of owning a great yacht if you couldn't walk along the deck in plain view of your friends—or even more important, in plain view of your enemies? And then there were the promenades at the new seaside resorts along the east and west coasts of the United States and in France. Designers started to show collections of beachwear. During the 1930s, railroads introduced special trains that would take people to the beach, and real estate developers began building beachfront resorts. Bathing suits became more revealing, and for the first time in history it was suddenly fashionable to have a tan.

But when a suntan turns into a sunburn, you've got a problem. This became an increasingly significant issue during the Second World War for our troops fighting in North Africa and the Pacific. The United States government felt they had to come up with *something* that would protect the skin of our soldiers.

The agent that seemed to work the best was a red pigment that was left as a residue after gasoline was extracted from crude oil. One of the people working on this experiment was a man named Dr. Benjamin Green.

Dr. Green believed that there was a huge market for a product that would protect people from the sun and at the same time help give them a tan. After the war, he took the technology that he had helped develop and produced a creamy white suntan lotion scented with jasmine. The product gave the user a copper-colored skin tone, which led Dr. Green to call his new invention Coppertone.

Nut-Crusted Pork Tenderloin

About hazel trees. The hazel tree is a low-growing shrub that dates back to 4500 B.C. The filbert tree is the domesticated hazel tree, but the nuts are the same for cooking purposes. The nuts of the filbert tree become ripe in late August, on or about the twentieth, which is St. Philbert's Day, hence the name.

1   TO COOK THE TENDERLOINS: Preheat the oven to 450° F. In 3 separate shallow bowls, place the nuts, flour, and egg. Dip the pork pieces, on all sides, including the ends, in each bowl, making sure to coat the tenderloins completely with the nuts. In a 10-inch skillet over moderate heat, heat the vegetable oil and sauté the pork on all sides until it's golden brown. Transfer the browned pork to a baking pan and roast for 20 to 25 minutes, or until the internal temperature of the pork reaches 160° F.

2   TO MAKE THE SAUCE: While the tenderloins are cooking, in a saucepan, combine the mango pulp, chicken stock, and cream, if using, and season with salt and pepper. Simmer over low heat until hot.

3   TO MAKE THE GARNISH: In a large skillet, heat the butter and sauté the bell peppers for a minute. Add the snow peas to the peppers, cover the skillet, and steam over low heat for a minute or two, or until the vegetables are cooked through but still crisp; season with salt and pepper.

4   TO SERVE THE TENDERLOIN: Cut the tenderloins into ½-inch slices and center a few slices on each plate. Top the pork with sautéed snow peas and red peppers and spoon the mango sauce around the pork.

Rum Point Club Restaurant, Cayman Islands

1½ cups finely ground nuts, such as macadamias, pecans, or hazelnuts, or a combination (see Notes)

¼ cup flour

1 egg, beaten with 2 tablespoons milk

Two 12-ounce boneless pork tenderloins, each cut in half

2 tablespoons vegetable oil

2 cups fresh or canned mango pulp (see Notes)

2 cups chicken stock

½ cup light cream (optional)

Salt and freshly ground black pepper to taste

2 tablespoons butter

2 red bell peppers, seeded and cut into fine julienne

½ pound snow peas

NOTES: To grind the nuts, put them in a food processor and pulse them until finely ground; do not overdo this step or the nuts will turn oily and pasty.

To make fresh mango pulp, peel and seed 4 ripe mangoes and puree in a blender or food processor. Add some of the chicken stock and puree until smooth.

Honey-Glazed Pork with Garlic Mashed Potatoes

2 pork tenderloins (total weight 1¾ pounds)

⅓ cup honey

2 tablespoons soy sauce

2 teaspoons Chinese five-spice powder

6 medium Idaho potatoes, peeled and cut into ½-inch dice

6 whole cloves garlic, peeled

3 to 6 tablespoons butter, plus 4 tablespoons cold butter

3 to 6 tablespoons half and half

Salt and freshly ground black pepper to taste

Sticky measuring. When you have to measure honey, molasses, corn syrup, or other sticky liquids, coat the surface of the measuring tool with a little butter or corn oil. The liquid will pour out easily, and you will have a more accurate measure.

1   Preheat the oven to 450° F. Set the pork tenderloins in a roasting pan and roast for 15 minutes. While they are roasting, in a small mixing bowl, combine the honey, soy sauce, and Chinese five-spice powder.

2   After 15 minutes, remove the pork from the oven, baste the tenderloins with the honey sauce, lower the heat to 350° and return them to the oven. Continue to roast, basting on occasion with the honey sauce, for 35 to 45 minutes, or until the internal temperature reaches 155° on an instant-read thermometer.

3   In a medium saucepan, place the potatoes and garlic covered by 2 inches of cold water. Simmer, partially covered, for 25 minutes, or until the potatoes are tender.

4   Drain the potatoes and return them to the pot, off the heat. Add 3 to 6 tablespoons of butter and half and half to the potatoes (add as little or as much as you like) and mash them with a masher or potato ricer. Or, puree the potatoes in a food mill (do not use a food processor; this will turn the potatoes gummy), and then whisk in the butter and half and half. Season with salt and pepper. Keep the potatoes warm in a double boiler until serving time or reheat right before serving in a microwave oven.

5   When the pork is done, transfer the tenderloins to a cutting board. Pour the pan and basting juices into a skillet and boil them down until ¾ cup remains. Remove the sauce from the heat and whisk in the cold butter, tablespoon by tablespoon; season with salt and pepper.

6   Cut the tenderloins on a diagonal into thin slices and set them on a plate; garnish with mashed potatoes. Brush 2 to 3 tablespoons of sauce over the pork slices.

Lemaire Restaurant, Jefferson Hotel, Richmond, Virginia

Richmond, Virginia

The Favorite Foods of Chicago: Italian Beef Sandwiches, Chicago-Style Pizza, and Hot Dogs

*T*HE stockyards made Chicago the beef capital of the world, which is presently reflected in its love of steaks, hot dogs, and Italian beef sandwiches.

The authentic Italian beef sandwich is made from roast beef that has been cooked with herbs and spices, cut thin, dunked in *au jus,* covered with sweet peppers, and served on Italian bread.

Chicago-style pizza was created by Ike Sole. He wanted to create a pizza that was more than a snack. He came up with a deep dish pizza that's a meal by itself.

The authentic Chicago-style hot dog starts as an all-beef sausage in a natural casing that snaps when you bite it. It's grilled or boiled—boiling keeps in the juices—and they're served on a steamed poppy-seed bun. But that's just the foundation. Chicago's history as the home of the skyscraper seems to have affected its approach to hot dogs. Yellow mustard goes on, then green relish, chopped raw onions, a slice of pickle, peppers, and finally tomatoes. This is as much about construction as it is about cooking.

And there is an "art" to naming a Chicago hot dog stand: Relish the Thought; Red Hot Mammas; Dog Day Afternoon; Wiener's Circle; and Mustard's Last Stand.

The Food Giants of Chicago

CHICAGO'S location made it the transportation hub for America's agricultural heartland, which in turn made it a center for food processing.

The Chicago Union Stockyards opened on Christmas Day in 1865, and were big enough to hold 10,000 head of cattle and 100,000 hogs. In those days, our nation was more interested in pork than beef. At first, the yard just fattened and shipped live cattle, but when Gustavus Swift arrived from New England, he started slaughtering and packing the beef and shipping it across the country in a new invention—the refrigerated railroad car.

At first, the railroads tried to stop him because they made more money shipping a live cow, but he was too swift for them and eventually won out.

The salt needed to preserve meat in the days before refrigeration made Chicago a salt trading center, which led to Chicago's Morton Salt Company.

In 1879, a man named John Stuart moved his mill from Canada to Chicago. Today, that mill is known as the Quaker Oats Company.

William Wrigley was a baking powder salesman. And every time you gave William an order, he threw in a free piece of chewing gum. Unfortunately, the baking powder business was failing, but everybody loved William's gum. So, in 1906, he went out of the baking powder business and into the gum business and introduced Wrigley's Spearmint.

PASTA, RICE, AND POTATOES

Bucatini all' Amatraciana

Linguine Puttanesca

Fettuccine Hunter's Style

Rigatoni with Mixed Grilled Vegetables

Spaghetti in Garlic-Tomato Sauce

Spaghetti Pecorino Romano

Scallops over Pasta

Lasagne with Smoked Cheese

Skillet Spanish Rice

Mozzarella Rice

Rice Pilaf

Spiced Rice and Beans

Pineapple Rice

The Food of Rome

*A*NCIENT Roman civilization covered a time period that lasted over a thousand years, with Rome itself starting out as a small agricultural community, and eventually becoming the capital of an empire that controlled most of what is now Western Europe, England, the Middle East, and North Africa. In the process, Rome evolved from a self-sufficient village that produced almost everything that its inhabitants ate and drank, into a magnificent city that imported its foods from around the world.

The ancient Romans liked meat, but most of it came from pigs, goats, and sheep. Cattle were considered as animals for commerce not cooking, and the work of cattle made their meat tough. There was lots of wild game and poultry, and hens were raised for their eggs. As a matter of fact, an egg dish was the most common first course at an ancient Roman meal.

The kitchen of the average ancient Roman family was rather limited in terms of size and equipment. A rectangle of bricks, set against one wall, was the oven and range. If the family could afford it, they burned charcoal rather than wood because charcoal gave off less smoke than firewood. A couple of holes in the top of the oven would hold the pots and pans, which were made of ceramic or bronze. There were also grills that look just like the grills we use today.

In most ancient societies everybody ate and drank pretty much the same things. Of course, the rich had a lot more of whatever it was than the poor. But in ancient Rome, perhaps for the first time, that began to change. Because the Roman Empire was so huge and in contact with so many different parts of the world, the people of ancient Rome who had money were able to choose from an extraordinary variety of foods. But they were not just interested in variety, they were fascinated by quality, and they would spend an enormous amount of time, money, and effort getting the best of everything.

That desire for the "best of class" is still very much part of the attitude of the modern Roman food lover. One of the first things that you learn as a traveling eater is that almost every town has a special interest in certain foods. Those same foods may be available in other cities but not at the same level of quality, and not subject to the same level of interest on the part of the local public.

Bucatini all'Amatraciana

One of the Oldest Vegetables. The ancient Egyptians believed that the onion was the symbol of the universe and would place their hand on an onion when they took an oath. Greek and Roman soldiers were fed onions to make them brave. The onion gets its name from the Latin word *unio,* which means the uniting of things in one, a reference to the many layers of an onion.

1 pound plum tomatoes; or 40 cherry tomatoes; or 1½ cups chopped, drained, canned plum tomatoes

¼ cup olive oil

1 cup finely chopped onions

2 cups finely diced Italian pancetta or bacon

¼ to ½ teaspoon crushed red pepper flakes

1 cup dry white wine or dry Vermouth

Salt to taste

1 gallon salted water

1 pound bucatini pasta or spaghetti

¼ cup freshly grated Parmesan cheese, plus extra for serving

2 tablespoons grated Pecorino cheese

1   If you are using fresh tomatoes, slice them in half and, with your hands, press out the seeds and liquid through a sieve set over a small bowl. Chop the flesh into ½-inch pieces. Press the seeds and liquid through the strainer to retrieve the tomato juices and reserve them for later.

2   In a 4-quart saucepan, heat the oil. When hot, add the onions and cook for 5 minutes, or until they're golden. Add the pancetta or bacon and cook for 2 to 3 minutes. Add the crushed red pepper and white wine and boil, over high heat, until half the liquid remains. Add the tomatoes and reserved juices and simmer for 15 minutes over low heat, or until the oil separates from the tomato juice. Season lightly with salt and add more crushed red pepper if you wish.

3   While the sauce is cooking, bring the water to a boil in a large pot. Add the bucatini pasta and cook for 10 minutes or until al dente (cooked through but still firm to the tooth). Right before draining, remove ¼ cup of cooking water and reserve.

4   Drain the bucatini and immediately add it to the sauce pot, off the heat. Toss it with the sauce and the reserved cooking water. Add the cheese and toss thoroughly. Adjust the seasoning and serve immediately with more cheese on the side.

The Excelsior Hotel, Rome, Italy

Nevada's Hot Spots

THE first people to live in the Nevada desert took up residence about 13,000 years ago. They lived in caves and dined on mammoths, with the sauce on the side. None of their recipes have survived, but the land they lived on is pretty much intact and absolutely amazing.

The Valley of Fire State Park is just north of Las Vegas and well worth the hour drive. This is the great American Southwest, and to come to Las Vegas and miss Petroglyph Canyon Trail is to miss half of what this place is really about. The highest formations are made of sand that was blown into the area about 150 million years ago. The dunes petrified into extraordinary shapes.

The petroglyphs are rock carvings that were put here by ancient tribes. They predate any of the known native cultures of North America and no one knows why they are here or what they mean. Some anthropologists believe that they were part of a prehunt ritual . . . kind of a combination pregame play plan and a pep talk by the head coach. Whatever they are, they are certainly in a magical setting.

The Valley of Fire State Park, Nevada

Linguine Puttanesca

About Capers. Capers are the pickled flower buds of the shrubbery caper plant, which grows wild in the countries that border the Mediterranean Sea. The best capers are the tiny nonpareils. The larger capers are very tasty but are stronger in flavor than the nonpareils and need to be chopped for most recipes. Capers are also available salted and dried.

1 TO PREPARE THE SAUCE: In a saucepan large enough to accommodate the sauce and the pasta, over medium heat, add the oil. Add the garlic and cook for a few seconds, or just until it begins to turn golden. Add the tomatoes and chicken stock and simmer for 2 to 3 minutes, just to heat through. Keep the sauce in the pan off the heat.

2 TO COOK THE PASTA: While the sauce is cooking, bring the salted water to a boil in a large pot. Add the linguine and cook for about 8 minutes, or until it's tender but still firm to the bite.

3 TO FINISH THE PASTA: Drain the linguine and return it to the sauce in the pot off the heat. Toss the linguine with the tomato sauce, black olives, capers, and parsley and season with salt and red pepper flakes.

Antonio's, Las Vegas, Nevada

¼ cup olive oil

2 large cloves garlic, or more to taste, thinly sliced

2 cups chopped canned plum tomatoes

½ cup chicken stock

4 quarts salted water

1 pound dry linguine or spaghetti

½ to 1 cup minced pitted black olives

2 tablespoons chopped capers

¼ cup finely chopped fresh Italian parsley

Salt to taste

⅛ teaspoon dried red pepper flakes

Fettuccine Hunter's Style

3 quarts salted water

¾ pound fresh fettuccine, preferably spinach

¼ cup olive oil

1 tablespoon chopped garlic

2 cups chopped portobello mushrooms (stems removed)

¼ cup julienned sun dried tomatoes

¼ cup Marsala

1 cup seeded and chopped fresh plum tomatoes

Salt and freshly ground black pepper to taste

¼ cup basil leaves, shredded by hand

2 cups (4 ounces) freshly grated Parmesan cheese

About Marsala. Marsala is a brownish sweet red wine that tastes of caramelized sugar. Made in the northeastern part of Sicily near the town of Marsala, it is blended from aromatic white wine, ground dried grapes, and brandy, then matured in oak casks for 2 to 5 years.

1 In a large pot bring the water to a boil. Add the fettuccine and cook for a few minutes, or until it's tender.

2 In a large skillet over medium heat, heat the olive oil. Sauté the garlic for 10 seconds. Add the mushrooms and cook for 2 to 3 minutes, or until they are somewhat tender. Add the sun-dried tomatoes and Marsala and boil for a minute, or until the wine has almost evaporated.

3 Add the tomatoes to the skillet, simmer for a minute to heat through, and season with salt and pepper.

4 Drain the fettuccine and return it to the cooking pot which is off the heat. Add the sauce to the fettuccine along with the basil and cheese. Toss well to combine and serve immediately.

Pasta & Pani, Virginia Beach, Virginia

Rigatoni with Mixed Grilled Vegetables

About Parmesan Cheese. Parmesan is a hard grating cheese that is made in and around the Italian city of Parma. True Parmesan cheese is labeled by Italian law as Parmigiano-Reggiano (and comes from the Emilia-Romagna region). Parmesan cheese is made from cow's milk and is aged 2 to 3 years. It is made in huge wheels that can weigh as much as 88 pounds.

Parmesan is a sharp, salty, tangy cheese, and when young, delicious as a table cheese. It is best to buy whole chunks of Parmesan and grate it yourself as you need it. You don't know how old pregrated Parmesan is, and it will continue to lose flavor rapidly. Grated Parmesan should be kept in the refrigerator and then warmed to room temperature for serving.

Keeping a whole chunk of Parmesan cheese fresh is easy. Wrap the cheese in a lightly damp cheesecloth or thin muslinlike cloth. Wrap that in aluminum foil and keep it in the refrigerator.

1 TO MARINATE THE VEGETABLES: In a large mixing bowl, combine the olive oil, oregano, and garlic, with 1 teaspoon of salt and ½ teaspoon of black pepper. Toss this with the vegetables and marinate at room temperature for at least an hour.

2 TO GRILL THE VEGETABLES: Prepare your charbroiler as you ordinarily would and grill the vegetables, in batches, until tender. Or, preheat your broiler and broil the vegetables, turning them once, until browned on both sides. (You can also set your oven to 500°F. and roast the vegetables for 30 minutes.) If you think the pieces are too large for pasta, then cool the vegetables for 10 minutes and chop them into manageable pieces.

3 In a large pot: Bring the salted water to a boil. Add the rigatoni and cook for about 12 minutes, or until it's tender but still firm to the bite. Drain, toss with the vegetables, basil, and Parmesan cheese. Season with salt and pepper, and serve immediately.

The Naples Beach Hotel and Golf Club, Naples, Florida

¼ cup olive oil

1 teaspoon chopped fresh oregano, or ½ teaspoon dried

2 cloves garlic, minced

1 teaspoon salt, plus extra to taste

½ teaspoon freshly ground black pepper, plus extra to taste

1 large (12 ounces) zucchini, sliced into ¼-inch rounds

1 large (12 ounces) yellow squash, sliced into ¼-inch rounds

1 red onion, peeled and cut into ¼-inch round pieces

8 to 10 ounces mushrooms, trimmed, wiped clean, and sliced vertically in half, or quarters if large

1 red bell pepper, seeded and cut into ½-inch strips

1 green bell pepper, seeded and cut into ½-inch strips

1 pound dry rigatoni pasta

¼ cup chopped fresh basil

1 cup grated Parmesan cheese

Spaghetti in Garlic-Tomato Sauce

3 quarts salted water

1 pound dry spaghetti

3 tablespoons olive oil

6 cloves garlic, smashed

1 large tomato, chopped

¼ cup chopped fresh basil leaves

2 cups favorite tomato sauce

*Salt and freshly ground black pepper
    to taste*

About "Spaghetti." Pasta is an ancient dish that probably got its start in China. But it was the Italians, from Naples, who became big fans of spaghetti, and who brought pasta to America.

Until recently, spaghetti was a generic term used to describe a dish composed of boiled stringy noodles and a zesty tomato sauce. The name spaghetti comes from the Italian word *spago,* which means "string." Today, spaghetti is just one of dozens of popular pasta shapes.

Flat pasta shapes like ravioli and fettuccine are commonly made from freshly rolled dough. Spaghetti and other round shapes are extruded through special dies and dried for an extended period.

1 In a large pot, bring the water to a boil. Cook the pasta for 8 to 10 minutes, or until it's tender but not soft. Drain and set aside.

2 In a large sauté pan over medium-high heat, heat the olive oil. Add the garlic and cook for 5 minutes, until cooked through and translucent, but not burned. Remove from the heat and let the garlic infuse with oil for 5 minutes. Add the tomato, basil, tomato sauce, salt, and pepper and heat through. Add the drained pasta to the sauce and toss to combine.

Remi Restaurant, New York City

Spaghetti Pecorino Romano

Makes 4 servings

About Pecorino cheese. In Italy, Pecorino cheese is made from sheep's milk—the Italian word for sheep is *pecora*. About 15 percent of the cheese made in Italy is Pecorino.

Fresh Pecorino Romano is a pungent table cheese. When it is aged and hard, it is the favored grating cheese of southern Italians. The hard grating Pecorino cheese of Sardinia is called "Sardo." Fresh Pecorinos are made all over Italy but they are highly perishable and rarely exported.

1 cup grated Pecorino Romano cheese
4 tablespoons freshly ground black pepper
4 quarts water
1 pound spaghetti
2 tablespoons olive oil (optional)

1   In a large bowl, put the Pecorino Romano cheese and toss with the pepper (there should be enough pepper flecks to speckle the cheese).

2   In a large pot, bring the salted water to a boil. Add the spaghetti and cook until just done. Drain the spaghetti, reserving ¾ cup of the water.

3   Add the pasta to the bowl of cheese and toss, adding the water it was cooked in if it is necessary to keep the spaghetti moist. Drizzle with olive oil, if desired, and serve.

Balducci's, New York City

Scallops over Pasta

3 quarts salted water

12 ounces dry fettuccine

1½ pounds sea scallops

2 tablespoons butter

¼ cup flour

½ cup regular or low-fat sour cream

*½ cup plus 2 tablespoons finely chopped
   fresh chives*

½ cup salmon caviar

1   In a large pot over high heat, bring the salted water to a boil. Add the fettuccine and cook for about 10 minutes, or until it's cooked through but still firm to the bite.

2   Meanwhile, prepare the scallops by pulling off the little piece of muscle attached to one side. Rinse under cold water and pat dry.

3   In a large non-stick skillet over medium heat, melt the butter. Set the flour in a shallow bowl or on a plate. Dip only one side of the scallops into the flour and shake off any excess. When the butter has melted, set the scallops, floured side down, in the skillet in a single layer and cook, without moving, over medium heat for 3 minutes. Cover the skillet and cook for another 2 minutes, or until the scallops are just cooked through.

4   Drain the pasta and return it to the pot, off the heat. Toss it with the sour cream, ½ cup of the chives, and the salmon caviar. Set a nest of pasta in the center of each plate and top each pasta nest with the scallops, set sautéed side facing up. Garnish each plate by surrounding the pasta with a dusting of the chives.

Bryggen Restaurant, Trondheim, Norway

Lasagne with Smoked Cheese

Makes 8 servings

Noodle notes. The Chinese have been eating noodles for 7,000 years and it may well be that pasta was first brought to Italy by the Ostrogoths, a Teutonic tribe that invaded Italy in the year 405. It is from their word *nudel* that we get ours. Noodles were noted in Italy by a Roman soldier named Ponzio Bastone 13 years before Marco Polo returned from the Orient, but Marco Polo generated a renewed interest in the food.

1 TO PREPARE THE SAUCE: In a medium skillet over medium heat, heat the olive oil. Crumble the beef into the skillet and cook, stirring, for about 5 minutes, or until the meat is no longer pink. Add the prepared sauce and bring to a simmer, then remove from the heat and set the sauce aside.

2 Preheat the oven to 375°F. In a large mixing bowl, combine the ricotta cheese with the egg and set aside.

3 TO ASSEMBLE THE LASAGNE: Spread 1 cup of the sauce in the bottom of a 9-×13-inch baking pan. Place 3 pieces of the uncooked lasagne pieces vertically, down the length of the pan, without them touching (they are precooked and will expand in the oven). Spread a third of the ricotta cheese mixture over the lasagne pieces, then one third of the grated Jarlsberg, then ½ cup of the remaining sauce. Repeat this procedure 3 times, making sure that each time you entirely cover the lasagne pieces with sauce and filling or they will dry out in the oven rather than rehydrate and become soft.

4 Spread the remaining sauce over the last 3 lasagne pieces, covering them well. With a vegetable peeler, shave very thin slices of the smoked cheese and place them over the tomato sauce. Cover the dish with foil and bake for 30 minutes. Remove the foil and bake for 15 minutes longer. Remove from the oven and let stand for 5 minutes before cutting.

Kafe Gasa, Trondheim, Norway

1 tablespoon olive oil

1 pound ground beef

4 cups prepared spaghetti sauce, such as marinara

One 15-ounce container of part-skim ricotta cheese

1 egg, lightly beaten

½ pound (12 pieces) "instant" or "oven ready" lasagne noodles (precooked and dry)

2 cups grated Jarlsberg cheese

2 ounce chunk smoked Jarlsberg cheese

La Mansion del Río, San Antonio, Texas

SITUATED directly on the banks of the San Antonio River is a building that has been designated a historic treasure. Planning for the main structure was started sixteen years after the fall of the Alamo by four brothers of the Society of Mary who arrived in San Antonio to build a school. In the 1930s, it became the home of St. Mary's University School of Law.

When the law school moved to a larger campus in 1966, the property was purchased by a graduate of the school named Patrick Kennedy. Pat's intention was to renovate the site and turn it into an elegant hotel. But this was his old law school and he loved the place. As he walked through the structure, he remembered his experiences and made sure that the design of the new building would conserve the old building.

The restored structure is known as La Mansion del Rio. The main restaurant is named Las Canarias. The name pays tribute to a group of settlers that came to San Antonio from the Canary Islands in 1723. And their namesake restaurant makes a significant contribution to the local gastronomy.

Skillet Spanish Rice

About rice. Rice first came to Texas hundreds of years ago with the Spanish. As a commercial product, it showed up in Texas right after the War Between the States. And the same things that made rice important then are the things that make rice important today. White rice has an almost unlimited shelf life. And brown rice will hold for about 6 months.

All rice is easy to cook. It's high in complex carbohydrates, which makes it one of the healthiest fuels for your body. It has a neutral flavor, which allows it to blend with other foods. And it is inexpensive. On a more modern note—it has no fat, no cholesterol, and no sodium.

1 pound lean ground beef

2 medium onions, chopped

½ green bell pepper, seeded and diced

1 cup uncooked white rice

1 teaspoon chili powder

½ teaspoon salt

½ teaspoon ground cumin

½ teaspoon freshly ground black pepper

1 cup tomato sauce, or one 8-ounce can tomato sauce

2 cups water

1   In a large skillet over medium heat, brown the ground beef, onions, and pepper; drain off the fat.

2   Stir in the remaining ingredients and bring to a boil. Reduce the heat, cover, and simmer for 20 minutes, or until the rice is tender.

San Antonio, Texas

Mozzarella Rice

2 cups cooked medium-grain rice

1½ cups shredded part-skim milk mozzarella cheese

¾ teaspoon dried basil, crushed

¼ teaspoon dried oregano, crushed

1 clove garlic, finely minced

1 cup vegetable or tomato juice

1 tablespoon chopped fresh parsley, or ½ tablespoon dried

About mozzarella cheese. Mozzarella is a soft fresh cheese usually used to top pizza. Most mozzarella is made from cow's milk, but the most authentic is made in Italy from the milk of water buffalo. Buffalo mozzarella has a tangier taste than mozzarella made from cow's milk.

The cheese is usually shaped like a baseball, but when very fresh, it may be too soft to hold a shape. It is sweet, slightly tangy, and creamy tasting, with a springy, pillowlike texture. Fresh mozzarella and packaged mozzarella are two very different products. Both have the essence of fresh whole milk in their flavor, but fresh mozzarella is preferable.

1 Preheat the oven to 350°F. Butter a 1-quart baking dish.

2 In the baking dish, combine the rice, ½ cup of the cheese, basil, oregano, garlic, and the juice. Stir to combine. Top with the remaining cup of cheese. Sprinkle with parsley.

3 Bake for 15 minutes, or until the cheese is melted and lightly browned. Serve immediately.

San Antonio, Texas

Rice Pilaf

About sage. Sage is a flavorful leafy perennial herb that comes primarily from the Mediterranean. The sage plant grows to a height of 2 feet and has 2-inch silvery-green leaves that are used fresh or dried.

British cooking is partial to sage, which is used to flavor pork sausages called "bangers" and as the color and subtle flavor in green Lancashire cheese.

The Chinese drink sage tea, and many people believe that sage helps promote a long and healthy life.

1 In a large, heavy saucepan over medium-high heat, heat the oil. Add the onions and sauté until they're soft and golden, 4 to 5 minutes.

2 Add the nuts and raisins and cook, stirring, for 1 minute more. Add the rice, and stir to coat with the oil. Cook for 3 to 4 minutes, until the rice begins to turn opaque, stirring constantly. Add the remaining ingredients and mix thoroughly.

3 Bring to a boil and reduce the heat to low. Cover and simmer for about 20 minutes, until the rice is tender but firm. Remove from the heat and place a clean towel taut over the top of the pan. Cover again for 5 minutes. The towel will absorb any remaining moisture.

Russian Tea Room, New York City

4 tablespoons vegetable oil

2 medium onions, chopped

⅓ cup pine nuts

⅓ cup golden raisins, plumped in hot water and drained

2 cups long-grain white rice

4 cups chicken stock

2 tomatoes, seeded and chopped

¼ cup chopped fresh parsley

1 teaspoon ground sage, crushed

½ teaspoon ground coriander

¼ teaspoon ground cinnamon

Freshly ground black pepper to taste

Early Immigration to the Bahamas

DURING the 1600s, the King of England was also the head of the Anglican Church. He believed that everyone should follow his religious regulations. The Puritan congregations, however, preferred to follow God without the King as middle man. The King made life difficult for the Puritans, and many of them decided to look for a new place to live. Some of the Puritans who left England ended up on Plymouth Rock and founded Massachusetts. The Puritans who were already in Bermuda were also being persecuted by the English government, and they escaped to the Bahamas. In 1647, they formed the first permanent settlement of Europeans in the islands.

The next meaningful migration took place during the last decades of the 1700s. It was made up of American colonists who had decided to stay loyal to the King of England and wanted to have nothing to do with the newly formed United States of America. The Loyalists who arrived came with their slaves and enhanced the racial mixture of the islands. In 1843, the British Empire abolished slavery, and much to the credit of all the Bahamians, there was an easy transition to a British colony made up of free citizens.

In 1973, after more than 250 years under British rule, the Bahamas became an independent nation. Today, it has a democratically elected government, a stable society, and a prospering economy.

Spiced Rice and Beans

About Tarragon. Tarragon is a relative newcomer to the herb scene. It is native to southern Russia and has only been cultivated for about 500 years. Tarragon is a feathery perennial that is impossible to grow from seed, which is one reason why it is not very popular in herb gardens. The long slender stems can be immersed in white wine vinegar to make tarragon vinegar. Both fresh and dried tarragon have a soft, near-sweet flavor.

1 TO PREPARE THE BEANS: Pick over the beans to remove any stones or foreign material. Rinse the beans and soak them for 6 hours or overnight. Or you can use the quick-soak method: Place the beans in a pot of water to cover and bring to a boil; boil for 3 minutes. Remove the pan from the heat and let the beans rest for 1 hour in the cooking water. Proceed with recipe.

2 Discard the water in which the beans were soaked or cooked. Place the beans in a pot with fresh water to cover. Add the onion, garlic, bay leaf, and orange zest. Boil the beans for 5 minutes, then reduce the heat and simmer gently for 1½ to 2 hours, or until the beans are tender. If the water gets low during the cooking, add more to cover the beans. Season the beans with the salt and pepper, and keep them warm while the rice cooks. The beans can be cooked a day ahead, refrigerated, and reheated before serving.

3 TO COOK THE RICE: In a medium skillet, heat the oil. Add the onion and sauté it over medium heat for 10 to 15 minutes, or until it becomes chestnut brown. As the onion cools, it will get crispy. Spoon the onion out of the pan and drain it on a paper towel.

4 Sauté the rice in the onion oil, stirring it with a wooden spoon to coat the grains evenly with the flavored oil. Add the chicken broth, diced peppers, water, and salt. Bring to a boil, reduce the heat to a simmer, and cook, covered, for 15 to 18 minutes,

(continued)

For the Beans:

1 cup black beans

½ onion, peeled

1 clove garlic, peeled

1 bay leaf

1 large piece orange zest, about 1 × 3 inches

1 teaspoon salt

¼ teaspoon freshly ground black pepper

For the Rice:

¼ cup olive oil

½ onion, finely minced

1 cup uncooked long-grain white rice

1 cup chicken broth

¼ cup diced red bell pepper

¼ cup diced green bell pepper

1 cup water

½ teaspoon salt

2 teaspoons fresh tarragon; or ½ teaspoon dried, crushed

2 teaspoons minced fresh flat-leaf parsley

or until the rice is tender and all the broth has been absorbed. Don't stir the rice while it is simmering or it will cook unevenly.

5   TO SERVE: When the rice is cooked, fluff in the herbs with a fork. Make a ring of rice on a serving platter. Drain the beans, discard the bay leaf, and pour the beans into the center of the rice. Sprinkle with the reserved crispy onions and serve.

Seagrapes Restaurant, Nassau, Bahamas

Pineapple Rice

About Pineapple. Pineapples originally grew wild in the jungles of South America. The Europeans first learned of them after Christopher Columbus discovered the island of Jamaica, and Hawaii, thought of as a pineapple-growing area, actually got its first pineapple from Jamaica. Jamaica's national coat of arms has a pineapple on it, and the watermark on Jamaican money is a pineapple. When Columbus took pineapples back to Spain, they were called *piña de las Indias* (pinecones of the Indies). Portuguese traders took pineapples to Africa, India, and on to Hawaii.

Pineapple is naturally sweet. When you buy fresh pineapple, look for a yellow-gold color around the eyes and at the base. The old test of pulling a leaf out easily to prove ripeness is not valid. The best test is to smell the bottom. If you get the smell of pineapple, it is ripe. Pineapple should be firm but tender. Avoid pineapples that are soft or discolored. Nutritionally, pineapples have 75 calories per cup. They're low in sodium and high in vitamin C.

2 cups water

1 cup long-grain rice

One 4-ounce slice fresh pineapple

2 tablespoons olive oil

¼ cup finely chopped scallions, white and green parts

1 small clove garlic, minced

½ cup finely diced roasted red bell pepper (you can buy a jar of these already roasted)

¼ cup pineapple juice

Salt and freshly ground black pepper to taste

1   TO COOK THE RICE: In a saucepan, bring the water to a boil, add the rice, cover, and simmer for 17 minutes, or until the rice is done. Set aside.

2   TO PREPARE THE PINEAPPLE: While the rice is cooking, preheat a non-stick skillet until it is very hot. Add the pineapple slice and cook over high heat for about 2 minutes per side, or until the pineapple is brown. Remove from the skillet and cut the pineapple into a fine dice; reserve for later.

3   TO ASSEMBLE THE RICE: In a sauté pan, heat the oil for 30 seconds. Add the scallions and garlic and sauté for a minute, or until the scallions are tender. Add the pineapple, roasted red bell pepper, and pineapple juice and boil down until the liquid has almost entirely evaporated. Season with salt and pepper and stir this mixture into the cooked rice.

La Mansion Del Rio, San Antonio, Texas

VEGETABLES AND EGGS

Beets and Apples in a Balsamic Vinaigrette

Black Bean Cakes

Tuscan Beans

Spinach and Beans with Pecorino Romano

Dry-Fried String Beans

Stir-Fried Carrots

Warm Tomatoes Stuffed with Spicy Couscous

Cajun Coleslaw

Egg White Fruit Frittata

Braised Belgian Endives

The Count Rumford Stove

ONE of the most beautiful open spaces in Munich, Germany, is the 900-acre English Garden which sits in the center of town. It was constructed during the late 1700s as a park open to all, where people of different classes could come together in a relaxed and natural setting.

The idea came from a man named Ben Thompson. Thompson was born in Woburn, Massachusetts, in the middle of the 1700s. When the Revolutionary War broke out, he sided with the English and moved to Europe. He became friendly with the Prince of Bavaria, who gave him the title of Count Rumford. Everyone in Munich thinks of Rumford in connection with the park. But I think his greatest achievement took place when he developed the prototype for the modern kitchen stove.

Beets and Apples in a Balsamic Vinaigrette

1 In a pot of water to cover, boil the beets for 1 hour or longer, or until they're tender.

2 While the beets are boiling, combine the vinegar, oil, and onion in a mixing bowl and season well with salt and pepper.

3 When the beets are done, drain them and cool in running water, then cut off their tops and peel them. Cut the beets into ½-inch dice, toss with the dressing, and season with salt and pepper.

4 Peel, core, and cut the apple into ½-inch dice.

5 To serve each portion of salad, center some apple in the middle of the plate and spoon the beets around the apple. Garnish the plate with 3 teaspoons of relish set around the beets, if desired.

Hotel Rafael, Munich, Germany

2 pounds fresh beets, trimmed of all but ½ inch of their tops, washed but not peeled

⅓ cup balsamic vinegar

2 tablespoons vegetable oil

⅓ cup finely minced red onion

Salt and freshly ground black pepper to taste

1 large Granny Smith apple, washed

Sweet relish (optional)

Black Bean Cakes

2 cups cooked black beans;
    or one 19-ounce can, drained

¼ cup (packed) cilantro leaves

2 teaspoons ground cumin

2 teaspoons chili powder

½ teaspoon dried oregano

½ teaspoon salt

2 tablespoons sour cream

4 scallions, green and white parts,
    thinly sliced

½ red bell pepper, seeded and finely
    chopped

¼ cup (or more if needed) dry bread
    crumbs or dehydrated mashed potato
    flakes

2 tablespoons yellow cornmeal

2 tablespoons vegetable oil

Garnish: sour cream, chopped fresh
    cilantro, diced red bell pepper

About cornmeal. Cornmeal is available in 2 colors: yellow and white. The former is ground from yellow corn kernels, the latter from white corn. In cooking, they are interchangeable. If a recipe calls for yellow cornmeal, you can use white; the color is the only difference. Generally, yellow cornmeal is used in down-home-style foods and white cornmeal is used when a more refined presentation is desired.

1 In a food processor, puree the black beans with the cilantro leaves, cumin, chili powder, oregano, salt, and sour cream. Transfer the mixture to a mixing bowl and add the scallions, red bell pepper, and enough bread crumbs or mashed potato flakes to bind the mixture tightly.

2 Form the mixture into twelve 2-inch disks and dredge them in the cornmeal.

3 In a large non-stick skillet, heat the vegetable oil. Sauté the cakes for 2 to 3 minutes on each side or until the cornmeal is browned. Serve immediately garnished with sour cream, cilantro, and diced red bell pepper.

The Lucky Star, Virginia Beach, Virginia

Tuscan Beans

Makes 4 servings

1 In a bowl, cover the beans with cold water and soak overnight.

2 The next day, drain the beans and put them into a pot with fresh water that covers the beans by 4 inches. Lightly salt the water, add the celery, carrot, bay leaf, and onion halves stuck with the 2 whole cloves. Over high heat, bring to a boil, lower the heat and simmer until the beans are tender, 30 to 40 minutes. Discard the vegetables and let the beans cool in their cooking liquid.

3 In a medium sauté pan over medium heat, gently heat the olive oil. Add the garlic and half the herbs and sauté for 2 to 3 minutes, being careful not to brown the garlic. With a slotted spoon, add the beans to the pan, turning them in the oil for 2 minutes. Then add about 1½ cups of their cooking liquid. Stir in half of the Pecorino Romano cheese and the remaining herbs. Boil briskly, about 10 minutes, until the bean liquid reduces slightly to form a "sauce." If the beans are tender before the sauce thickens, remove them with a slotted spoon and continue boiling down the liquid, then pour over the beans. Add salt and pepper, if needed, and transfer the beans to a serving platter. Sprinkle the remaining cheese over the beans.

Union Square Cafe, New York City

1 cup dried cannellini beans

1 stalk celery

1 carrot, peeled and split lengthwise

1 bay leaf

1 medium white onion, peeled and halved

2 whole cloves

3 tablespoons olive oil

3 cloves garlic, finely chopped

1 teaspoon finely chopped fresh rosemary, or ½ teaspoon dried

1 teaspoon finely chopped fresh thyme, or ½ teaspoon dried

1 teaspoon finely chopped fresh sage, or ½ teaspoon dried

¾ cup grated Pecorino Romano cheese

Salt and freshly ground black pepper to taste

Spinach and Beans with Pecorino Romano

2 tablespoons olive oil

2 cloves garlic, crushed

1 pound spinach leaves, cleaned

One 16-ounce can cannellini or kidney
    beans or chick-peas rinsed and
    drained; or 2 cups cooked

Grating of Pecorino Romano cheese

About olive oil. Olive comes in three grades: extra virgin, which comes from the first pressing of the best olives; virgin, which comes from the second pressing; and pure, which is the lowest-quality olive oil.

The oil should be stored refrigerated in a dark and airtight container. If the oil gets cloudy or solid, just let it come back to room temperature and it will be fine.

1 In a large stockpot or skillet over medium-high heat, heat the olive oil. Add the crushed garlic and cook for 1 to 2 minutes, until it's golden.

2 Add the spinach leaves to the pot. Cover and cook for 3 to 4 minutes, until they're wilted, stirring once.

3 Add the cooked beans to the pot and cook for 1 to 2 minutes longer until heated through.

4 Serve with a grating of Pecorino Romano cheese.

Baja California, Mexico

Dry-Fried String Beans

About soy sauce. Soy sauce is made by fermenting boiled and ground soybeans, roasted barley, or cracked wheat with some salt. The Japanese use light soy sauce, the Chinese use soy sauce that is darker and stronger tasting, and Indonesian soy sauce is sweetened with molasses. In general, the high salt content of soy sauce keeps it from spoiling at room temperature, but refrigeration does not hurt the flavor.

From a nutritional standpoint, soy sauce should be used carefully by people on a low-sodium diet. One tablespoon of soy sauce can contain 1,479 milligrams of sodium. Some manufacturers make low-sodium soy sauce that contains only 605 milligrams of sodium per tablespoon.

1½ pounds string beans, trimmed

1 cup vegetable oil

1 tablespoon chopped scallions (green and white parts)

1 tablespoon chopped garlic

½ teaspoon Szechuan chili paste or hot sauce

2 tablespoons soy sauce

1 tablespoon dry sherry or rice wine

1 teaspoon sugar

1 Wash the beans under running water. Dry the beans well on paper towels.

2 In a wok or skillet, heat the oil until just before it smokes. Add the beans, standing back to avoid being spattered with oil. Cook the beans over high heat, stirring and turning frequently, until they are wrinkled and lightly browned, about 7 minutes. Remove the beans with a slotted spoon and place in a colander to drain. Set aside.

3 Discard all but about 2 tablespoons of oil from the skillet. Over high heat, reheat the remaining oil. Add the scallions, garlic, and Szechuan paste and stir-fry for 20 seconds. Add the soy sauce and stir.

4 Put the string beans back into the skillet. Add the wine and sugar and stir until well mixed, about 1 minute. Remove from the skillet and serve.

Shun Lee, New York City

Stir-Fried Carrots

1 pound carrots
2 tablespoons vegetable oil
4 slices gingerroot
¼ cup chicken stock
1 tablespoon soy sauce

About carrots and nutrition. Carrots contain carotene, which is changed by the liver into vitamin A. Vitamin A is necessary for healthy skin and mucous membranes, and promotes the proper functioning of our immune system. It also may be helpful in preventing certain types of cancer, such as lung and bladder cancer.

1 Peel the carrots and slice them into ¼-inch diagonal slices. Bring a pot of water to a boil and blanch the carrots for 5 minutes.

2 In a medium sauté pan over medium-high heat, heat the oil. Add the gingerroot and cook for 15 seconds. Add the drained carrots and stir-fry to coat with the oil.

3 Combine the stock and soy sauce and pour over the carrots. Simmer until the carrots are tender.

San Francisco, California

Warm Tomatoes Stuffed with Spicy Couscous

1 Preheat the oven to 350°F.

2 TO MAKE THE COUSCOUS: In a 1-quart saucepan, bring the chicken stock, water, tomato sauce, zucchini, carrot, garlic, and spices to a boil. Add the couscous. Lower the heat to medium and cook for 3 minutes, or until most of the water is absorbed and the couscous is fluffy. Cover, turn off the heat, and let steam for 2 minutes.

3 Stir in parsley and mix gently.

4 TO MAKE THE TOMATOES: Remove the tops of the tomatoes and scoop out the seeds and pulp. Slice a thin piece of the tomato so that it sits on a baking sheet without tilting.

5 Fill the hollowed tomatoes with the spicy couscous and bake for 10 minutes, or until they're warmed through.

6 TO SERVE: Top each tomato with grated lemon rind. Divide the zucchini slices on 6 plates in a circular pattern and place a filled tomato in the center of each plate.

Naples, Florida

For the Spicy Couscous:

1 cup chicken stock

½ cup water

¼ cup tomato sauce

½ cup finely diced zucchini

½ cup finely diced carrot

1 clove garlic, minced

½ teaspoon ground cumin

¼ teaspoon ground coriander

⅛ teaspoon allspice

¼ teaspoon freshly ground black pepper

Generous dash cayenne

½ cup couscous

2 tablespoons chopped parsley

For the Stuffed Tomatoes:

6 tomatoes

Grated lemon rind

1 zucchini, thinly sliced

Cajun Coleslaw

2 cups mayonnaise

1 tablespoon chopped fresh tarragon

3 tablespoons wine vinegar

¼ cup prepared hot mustard

¼ teaspoon celery seed

Freshly ground black pepper to taste

10 cups shredded green cabbage

1   In a bowl, blend together all of the ingredients except the cabbage.

2   Mix the dressing with the cabbage until all the cabbage is evenly coated with the dressing.

3   Refrigerate briefly before serving.

New Orleans, Louisiana

Egg White Fruit Frittata

Makes 1 serving

1 In a bowl, whip egg whites until they're almost stiff. Coat a 7-inch non-stick skillet or omelet pan with the low-fat spray and warm over medium heat. Add half of the fruit to the skillet and sauté, stirring, for about 30 seconds.

2 Add the egg whites and let them cook, without stirring, for 10 seconds. With a wooden spoon, move the egg whites around and cook for another 10 seconds, or until they're set and fully cooked (don't move them too much or you end up with scrambled egg whites).

3 Slide the frittata onto a dessert plate and spoon the remaining fruits over the top. Drizzle the fruit with honey, if desired, and dust lightly with confectioners' sugar.

Edgewater Beach Hotel, Naples, Florida

4 egg whites

Low-fat cooking spray

3 tablespoons ¼-inch cantaloupe dice

3 tablespoons ¼-inch honeydew dice

2 whole strawberries, trimmed and thinly sliced

10 blueberries

1 tablespoon raisins

½ banana, sliced

1 teaspoon honey (optional)

Confectioners' sugar as garnish (optional)

Braised Belgian Endives

12 endives
¼ teaspoon grated nutmeg
½ teaspoon salt
¼ teaspoon freshly ground black pepper
½ cup (1 stick) unsalted butter
1½ cups water

About endives. When the Belgian revolution broke out in 1830, Jan Lammers hid his crop of chicory roots in a dark basement and fled his farm near Brussels. When the short uprising ended and Lammers returned, he found that his chicory had sprouted white shoots. He was able to repeat the process and thereby began cultivating the first endives.

The endive is still grown on small farms around Brussels with techniques that are similar to the original process. An endive head contains about 15 calories, vitamins A, B_1, B_2, and C, as well as iron and potassium.

1   Preheat the oven to 325°F. Butter a casserole and a sheet of aluminum foil.

2   Trim ¼-inch off the end of each endive. Wash them in cold water and drain thoroughly in a colander. Cut an X in the base of each endive so that they will cook evenly.

3   In the casserole, arrange the endives in layers. Between each layer, sprinkle the endives with nutmeg, salt, and pepper, and dot with butter. Pour in the water and cover with the buttered aluminum foil.

4   Bake in the oven for 20 minutes, until the endives are tender, and serve.

Brussels, Belgium

SALADS

Green Bean and Potato Salad with a Bacon Vinaigrette

German-Style Potato Salad

Orange and Onion Salad

California Chicken Salad

Crabmeat Salad

Haddock on Caesar Salad

Warm Tuna Salad

The Grand Place of Brussels

THE Grand Place was once the main marketplace for the city of Brussels, a fact which is echoed in the names of the streets that lead into the square: Butter Street, Meat and Bread Street, and Herring Street. The square is surrounded by the guildhouses from which representatives of various crafts tried to influence government policy. The most powerful guild was made up of bakers, who were located in the buildings marked one and two. The golden head over their door is St. Aubert, the patron saint of bakers. The six figures above represent the elements needed to bake bread: energy, grain, wind, fire, water, and prudence. These days, the building houses one of the more popular bars where fire water and prudence are still matters of concern.

Green Bean and Potato Salad with a Bacon Vinaigrette

Makes 4 servings

A specialty of the Belgian town of Liège is a warm green bean and potato salad with a bacon vinaigrette. Potatoes and green beans still hot from the cooking pots are mixed with freshly sautéed bacon, then dressed with warm vinegar and shallots.

1 To a large pot, add the salted water. Boil the potatoes in their skins, covered, for 35 to 40 minutes, or until you can pierce them easily with a knife but they are not falling apart. Remove from the water with a slotted spoon and set aside in a large mixing bowl.

2 Add the green beans to the same water and boil for 5 minutes, or until they are tender yet still firm to the bite; drain but do not cool under running water; set aside in a separate mixing bowl.

3 As the green beans are boiling, in a medium skillet over medium heat, heat the oil and sauté the bacon strips, turning on occasion, for about 5 minutes, or until the bacon is brown and crisp. Remove the skillet from the heat.

4 Peel and slice the potatoes into ¼-inch rounds and add them to the green beans. Add the bacon bits and the rendered fat, along with the shallots or red onion, and vinegar, and toss until well combined. Season with salt and lots of freshly ground black pepper. Serve while warm.

Hotel Metropole, Brussels, Belgium

4 quarts salted water

½ pounds new potatoes, washed

12 ounces green beans, tails removed and cut into 2-inch lengths

2 tablespoons vegetable oil

¼ pound slab bacon, cut into 1-×-¼-inch strips

⅓ cup minced shallots or red onion

¼ cup white wine vinegar

Salt and freshly ground black pepper to taste

German-Style Potato Salad

2 pounds baking potatoes

⅛ cup vegetable oil

3 tablespoons cider vinegar

¾ cup beef stock

1 small onion, finely minced

Salt and freshly ground black pepper to
taste

¼ cup chopped fresh parsley for garnish

About Potatoes. The potato is probably the most widely used vegetable in the world. Potatoes are native to the mountains of northern South America, where Indians domesticated wild potatoes. Spanish conquistadors brought potatoes back to Europe where they became particularly popular as a crop for European peasants because they grew underground, well hidden from invading troops who regularly pillaged farms for food. Ireland was the first European country to cultivate potatoes; in time, the Irish diet became so dependent on potatoes that when the potato famine hit in 1845, thousands of people died and thousands more sailed to America to escape.

There are over 15 varieties of potatoes grown in the United States, but they can be separated into 4 major groups. The round white, also known as the Cobbler, Kennebec, and Katahdin, are good for good for boiling, frying, and baking. The round red or waxy red is very good for boiling. The long white potato is grown mainly in the western states and is good for boiling, frying, and baking. The long Russet or Burbank potato is considered by many as the best baking potato available.

The volcanic soil and climatic conditions make potatoes grown in Idaho among the best in the world. Nutritionally, potatoes are a very good source of dietary fiber. They are low in calories if you don't put butter and sour cream on them (a single Russet averages 100 calories), and they are a good source of vitamin C and potassium.

1 In a large saucepan over medium heat, put in the potatoes and cover them with water. Cook until tender, about 45 minutes. Remove the potatoes from the water and cool for 10 minutes, until they are easy to handle. Cut them into slices about ¼ to ½ inch thick.

2 Place the potatoes in a large shallow bowl and sprinkle with oil and vinegar. Add the stock and the onion. Season with salt and pepper. Toss the mixture gently.

3 Cover the bowl and let the mixture stand at room temperature for 2½ hours, tossing gently after 1 hour. This salad should not be chilled. Just before serving, garnish with parsley.

Boise, Idaho

Orange and Onion Salad

Lettuce leaves

2 oranges, peeled, pitted, and sliced

1 small red onion, peeled and thinly
sliced

¼ cup your favorite vinaigrette

½ red bell pepper, cored and cut into
strips

About oranges. The orange is a 20-million-year-old berry, and one of the most important fruits in world economics. Oranges are native to China, and were first planted in Europe by the Moors in the tenth century. Christopher Columbus brought oranges from the Canary Islands to the West Indies. Later they were planted in Panama, where the Aztec priests took excellent care of them. Oranges have been grown in Florida since the mid 1500s, and in California since 1769, when oranges were first planted by missionaries.

Oranges do not continue to ripen once they have been picked, and their orange color is not a sign of ripeness, but rather a reaction to cold weather. Look for oranges that are firm, heavy for their size, and smooth-skinned. Store them in a cool place. They are an excellent source of vitamins A and C, potassium, and folic acid.

1 Arrange the lettuce leaves on 2 serving plates. Arrange the oranges and the sliced onion in an attractive pattern on each plate.

2 Sprinkle 2 tablespoons vinaigrette over each salad and garnish with pepper strips.

Baja California, Mexico

California Chicken Salad

About Gruyère and Swiss cheese. Gruyère cheese has superb melting qualities that make it the best choice for many cooked dishes as well as fondues and soup toppings. The best Gruyère comes from Switzerland, and is sold by the piece. Avoid the tiny foil-wrapped triangles—they will not work well in most recipes.

Swiss cheese is a generic name for all imitations of the original Swiss Emmentaler.

1 In a large mixing bowl, toss the lettuce, chicken, Swiss, tomato, Cheddar, beets, and egg white.

2 In a small mixing bowl, combine the vinegar, mustard, chives, tarragon, Worcestershire, Tabasco, salt, and pepper. Pour in the oil in a thin stream, whisking to combine. Toss together with the salad and, if desired, garnish with the bacon. Serve immediately.

Regent Beverly Wilshire Hotel, Beverly Hills, California

4 cups chopped iceberg lettuce

1 cup diced cooked boneless, skinless chicken breast

½ cup diced Swiss cheese

1 tomato, chopped

½ cup diced Cheddar cheese

¼ cup diced cooked beets

1 hard-boiled egg white, diced

3 tablespoons red wine or favorite vinegar

1 tablespoon Dijon-style mustard

1 tablespoon chopped fresh chives

1 teaspoon fresh tarragon, or ¼ teaspoon dried, crushed

¼ teaspoon Worcestershire sauce

Tabasco sauce to taste

Salt and freshly ground black pepper to taste

¼ cup vegetable oil

Cooked crumbled bacon for garnish (optional)

Crabmeat Salad

1 pound cooked fresh lump crabmeat,
  cleaned to remove any shell

1 cup ¼-inch red bell pepper dice

¼ cup wafer-thin slices of red onion

1 teaspoon salt

1 teaspoon coarsely ground black pepper

¼ cup fresh lime juice

¼ cup white wine vinegar

¼ cup olive oil

4 ripe fresh tomatoes

8 large Boston lettuce leaves, washed,
  patted dry

1 pound fresh asparagus, cooked and
  chilled

2 hard-boiled eggs, peeled and cut into
  quarters

How the Limeys got their name. In the sixteenth, seventeenth, and eighteenth centuries, when the British navy ruled the waves, extended ocean voyages were typical. But the restricted diet of hardtack and salted meat left the sailors weak and sick from a disease called "scurvy." British navy doctors started giving the men limes to eat and their illnesses disappeared, though it was not quite clear at the time why this was so. Modern science has revealed that it was the vitamin C in the limes that kept the men healthy. Sailors from other countries noticed this peculiar habit among their English counterparts and began calling the English sailors "limeys."

1 TO MAKE THE SALAD: In a mixing bowl, combine the crabmeat, bell pepper, onion, salt, pepper, lime juice, vinegar, and olive oil and toss well. Cover and refrigerate until serving time.

2 TO MAKE THE TOMATO CUPS: Core each tomato, and on each one, make 4 incisions perpendicular to each other, but do not cut all the way through. Leave the tomato attached to the bottom. Gently pry the tomato points apart, thus forming a tomato crown with 8 wedges.

3 TO SERVE: Arrange each tomato crown on lettuce leaves and spoon the crabmeat salad in the middle; if it spills over the top that's okay. Garnish each plate with the cooked asparagus and hard-boiled eggs.

The Naples Beach Hotel and Golf Club, Naples, Florida

Haddock on Caesar Salad

Makes 6 servings

1 TO MAKE THE CAESAR SALAD DRESSING: In a blender or food processor, combine the garlic, lemon juice, Worcestershire sauce, and ½ cup olive oil. Puree until smooth. If you wish, add the anchovies and process just until chopped. Season with salt and pepper and set aside until later.

2 TO MAKE THE CROUTONS: Preheat the oven to 400°F. Set the French bread cubes on a baking sheet and bake for 10 to 12 minutes, or until they're golden. Remove from the oven and gently toss them with the tablespoon of olive oil; set aside until later.

3 TO MAKE THE TOPPING: In a food processor, combine the sun-dried tomatoes, ⅓ cup of Parmesan cheese, and dried bread crumbs and process until it has the consistency of coarse cornmeal. Set the haddock on a baking sheet and spread each steak with some of the sun-dried tomato coating.

4 Place the haddock into the oven and bake for about 10 minutes, or until it's just cooked through. Meanwhile, toss the romaine lettuce with all but 2 tablespoons of the dressing. Arrange some salad on each of the dinner plates and sprinkle the greens with a few croutons. When the fish is done, center it over the salad and drizzle each piece of fish with some dressing.

Radisson Hotel, Trondheim, Norway

¼ teaspoon minced garlic

3 tablespoons fresh lemon juice

1½ teaspoons Worcestershire sauce

½ cup plus 1 tablespoon olive oil

6 anchovy fillets (optional)

Salt and freshly ground black pepper to taste

6 slices French bread, cut into ½-inch cubes

½ cup plus ⅓ cup freshly grated Parmesan cheese

6 sun-dried tomatoes, packed in oil, drained and patted dry

¼ cup dried bread crumbs

Six 6-ounce haddock steaks

1 large head romaine lettuce, washed, dried, and torn into 1-inch pieces

Warm Tuna Salad

6 tablespoons olive oil

4 tablespoons vegetable oil

⅓ cup balsamic vinegar

2 tablespoons chopped capers

½ teaspoon kosher salt, plus extra
    to taste

Freshly ground black pepper to taste

Four 6- to 8-ounce fresh tuna steaks

2 medium all-purpose potatoes, each cut
    into 6 to 8 wedges

½ teaspoon dried thyme

1 teaspoon minced garlic

Twelve ¼-inch-thick slices unpeeled
    cucumber, cut on the bias

12 wedges hard-boiled eggs

2 cups mesclun or other greens, washed,
    dried, and torn into bite-sized pieces

Optional garnish: 2 cups deep-fried
    shredded sweet potatoes and lime
    wedges, or 2 tomatoes, diced and
    tossed with 1 tablespoon balsamic
    vinegar and 2 tablespoons shredded
    fresh basil

1 Heat the oven to 400°F.

2 In a bowl, combine 4 tablespoons of olive oil, 2 tablespoons of vegetable oil, the balsamic vinegar, and capers and season with salt and pepper. Marinate the tuna in 2 tablespoons of this dressing at room temperature.

3 Coat the potatoes with dried thyme, garlic, and the remaining 2 tablespoons of vegetable oil; season with ½ teaspoon of salt and the pepper. Roast the potatoes for 35 to 40 minutes, or until they're tender. Remove from the oven.

4 Set 3 slices of cucumber around the edge of each plate. In between the cucumbers, set wedges of roasted potato and hard-boiled egg.

5 In a bowl, toss the greens with 2 more tablespoons of the caper vinaigrette and set a pile of greens in the middle of each plate. Gently heat the remaining vinaigrette.

6 In a non-stick skillet over high heat, sauté the tuna steaks for 2 to 3 minutes per side and set them on top of the salad. Drizzle the warm vinaigrette over the tuna and the other ingredients. Top the tuna with fried sweet potatoes or diced tomatoes and basil, if desired.

Pink Sands, Harbour Island, Bahamas

top left: *Man Mo Temple, Hong Kong*
top right: *Hong Kong Harbor*
center: *Food store, Hong Kong*
above right: *Baby girl, Hong Kong*
left: *Chicken with Macadamia Nuts, Hong Kong*

PHOTOS BY BURT WOLF

top: *Chicken Stovies with Clapshot Sc*
far left: *Sc*
center: *Palace guard, Edinburgh Sc*
left: *Highlands Sc*
PHOTOS BY B■RT

FROGS
CROSSING
DRIVE
WITH CARE

top far left: *Biscotti, Milan*
top center: *Fashions, Milan*
above: *Chicken with Citrus Sauce, Milan*
left: *Minestrone alla Milanese, Milan*
below: *Rome*
PHOTOS BY BURT

above left: *Peck's Food Market, Milan, Italy*
above: *Food market, Rome, Italy*
left: *Lovers, Milan, Italy*
PHOTOS BY BURT WOLF

top left: *Munich, Germ*
top center: *Munich, Germ*
top right: *Munich, Germ*
left: *Pretzel Dumpling Soup, Munich, Germ*
above: *Cherries, Munich, Germ*

PHOTOS BY BURT W

top left: *Foods, Trondheim, Norway*
top right: *Making flatbread, Trondheim Folk Museum, Trondheim, Norway*
left: *Kafe Gasa, Trondheim, Norway*
bottom left: *Trondheim, Norway*
bottom right: *Trondheim, Norway*

PHOTOS BY BURT WOLF

top left: Street waffles, Brussels, Belg
above: Street waffles, Brussels, Belg
middle left: The Grand Place, Brussels, Belg
left: Beef Braised in Beer, Brussels, Belg

PHOTOS BY BURT W

CAKES, PIES, TARTS, AND COOKIES

Apple Tart with Licorice Sauce

Baked Alaska

Chocolate Cappuccino Tart

Killer Fudge Cake

Chocolate Brownies with Ice Cream and Kahlúa

Devil's Food Cake

Chocolate Surprise Cupcakes

Roman Cheesecake

Pecan-Apricot Cake

Pound Cake

Coconut Cake

Orange Angel Food Cake with Orange Glaze

Pear-Walnut Coffee Cake

Mango Strudel with Vanilla-Lime Sauce

Klondike Kate's Tin Roof Pie

Chocolate Sauce

Southern Pecan Pie

Caramelized Pineapple Upside-Down Tart

Egg White Angel Cake

Spoon Bread

Buttermilk Raisin Scones

Peanut Butter Cookies

High-Fiber Orange-Bran Muffins

High-Protein, High-Fiber, Low-Fat Egg White Pancakes

Blueberry Muffins

Lemon-Yogurt Muffins

Triple Berry Muffins

Fruit Tartlets

Figgy Duff

Apple Tart with Licorice Sauce

For the Dough:

1 cup all-purpose flour

Pinch salt

½ cup (1 stick) unsalted butter, chilled,
  cut into tablespoon-sized pieces

About 3 tablespoons iced cold water

For the Tart:

Flour for rolling out dough

3 Golden Delicious apples

2 tablespoons melted unsalted butter

3 tablespoons sugar

For the Licorice Sauce:

½ cup store-bought caramel or butterscotch sauce

½ cup water

2 teaspoons aniseed

Ice cream to serve with tart (optional)

1 TO MAKE THE DOUGH: In a food processor, combine the flour with a pinch of salt. Add the cold butter and pulse the machine 15 to 20 times, or until the butter has been cut into the flour in pieces about the size of oatmeal flakes. Keeping the machine running, add the water and process, pulsing the machine on and off, for a few seconds longer, or until the dough comes together. Transfer the dough to the counter. If it is still dry, sprinkle it with a teaspoon or so of water and work the water into the dough. Flatten the dough into a disk and chill, preferably overnight, or for at least 2 hours.

2 TO ROLL OUT THE DOUGH: Lightly flour the counter and roll out the dough into a circle approximately 12 inches in diameter and about ⅛ inch thick. Transfer the dough to a large baking sheet. Roll up the edges of the dough with your fingers to form a rim. Dip a fork in flour and crimp the rim with the fork to form a decorative edge. Then prick the entire surface of the pastry with the tines of the fork and refrigerate the dough while you prepare the apples.

3 TO PREPARE THE TART: Peel the apples and cut them in half vertically, along the axis of the core. Scoop out the cores. Place the apple halves on a cutting board, flat side down, then cut the apple halves into ⅛-inch-thick slices.

4 TO BAKE THE TART: Preheat the oven to 400°F. Remove the dough from the refrigerator. Press overlapping slices of apple in a circle against the outer rim of the pastry. Then press a second, smaller circle of overlapping slices inside the larger one and continue this way until the surface of the pastry is covered with apple slices. Drizzle the melted butter over the apples and sprinkle the sugar evenly over the butter. Bake for 40 to 45 minutes, or until the surface of the apples is golden brown.

5   TO MAKE THE SAUCE: While the tart is baking, transfer the caramel or butterscotch sauce into a small saucepan and add the water and aniseed; simmer for 5 minutes. Strain out the aniseed.

6   TO SERVE THE TART: Cool the tart for 10 minutes, then cut it into 6 large slices. Transfer each slice to a plate and drizzle on some of the sauce. Serve with ice cream if desired, and additional licorice sauce.

Restaurant Havfruen, Trondheim, Norway

Demonstration of traditional Norwegian folk instrument, open-air Folkmuseum, Trondheim, Norway

Helping You Feel at Home on the High Seas

*W*HEN luxury ocean liners first came on the scene at the beginning of the twentieth century, their owners wanted to market the first-class services to upper-class families. One of the simplest ways to work toward that goal was to reproduce on the ship that reminded the passengers of life on shore: a grand ballroom with a majestic staircase—a staircase that could be used by the female passengers to make a grand entrance in a magnificent new dress. The grand ballrooms were replicas of the famous hotel ballrooms in Paris and London.

The shipping companies put orchestras in the ballrooms—orchestras that everyone knew from the hotels, and they played music that was associated with good times.

There was also an endless supply of luxurious food that spoke of opulence and happiness. The shipping companies created an environment that felt like the important public events of a social season or an ongoing wedding party.

There were rooms that reminded the male passengers of the private clubs that were popular at the time. The passengers began to feel secure, even though they were hundreds of miles at sea.

Cruising Alaska aboard the Legend of the Seas

Baked Alaska

The key to success for this recipe is to keep the ice cream as cold as possible and turn up the oven as high as it will go.

1 Cut each pound cake into 3 horizontal slices; each slice should be about 9½ inches long, 2½ inches wide, and slightly thicker than ½ inch.

2 Set a slice of cake on a baking dish. Cut a piece of the block of ice cream to fit on the cake base, keeping ¾ inch clear all around. Return the cake and ice cream to the freezer for about an hour, or until the ice cream is hard again.

3 Remove the cake and ice cream from the freezer and fully enclose the ice cream with more slices of pound cake "glued" to the ice cream with jam. Return the cake and ice cream to the freezer for at least 2 hours.

4 Preheat the oven to its highest setting. Beat the egg whites until semi-stiff. Gradually add the sugar to the egg whites, a couple of tablespoonsful at a time, and continue to beat until the meringue is stiff and glossy.

5 Remove the ice cream and cake from the freezer. With a spatula, spread about half of the meringue over the pound cake, making sure to completely cover the sides and top. Transfer the remaining meringue to a pastry bag fitted with a star tip and pipe it over the cake, making it as decorative as you wish. Bake for 3 minutes to brown the meringue, and serve the Baked Alaska immediately so the ice cream doesn't melt.

Legend of the Seas, *Cruising Alaska*

Two 1-pound frozen pound cakes (Sara Lee)
Half gallon block of your favorite flavor ice cream
Apricot jam, as needed
8 egg whites
¾ cup "instant" superfine sugar

The Origins of Chicago

TWELVE thousand years ago, North America's midwest was covered with a huge glacial lake. As it receded, it left wide prairies, the Great Lakes, and shores of swamp. The marshlands that were at the southwest corner of what we presently call Lake Michigan were overgrown with wild onions—onions that gave off an intense odor. The native tribes called the place *Checagou,* which means "great strength."

Today, we call that spot "Chicago"—and it is stronger and sweeter than ever. Chicago is the most *American* city in the United States, and its importance lies in its location. To the north and east are the Great Lakes, and the St. Lawrence Seaway running out to the Atlantic Ocean. To the south is a network of rivers that join the Mississippi and flow down to the Gulf of Mexico. Chicago is the control point between these two waterways, and people have been using it as a central trading post for thousands of years.

The first permanent settler was Jean Baptiste Point DuSable. He was the son of a French-Canadian merchant and an African-American slave. In 1779, he set up a trading post on what eventually became the most important shopping street in Chicago: Michigan Avenue, also referred to as "the Magnificent Mile."

Chocolate Cappuccino Tart

1   TO PREPARE THE DOUGH: In a bowl with an electric mixer, beat the butter, sugar, and cocoa powder until they're well combined. Add the egg and egg yolk. Do not worry if the mixture looks curdled. In a separate bowl with a whisk, combine the flour, baking soda, and salt, then add this to the butter mixture and combine with your hands. Flatten the dough into a ½-inch disk, wrap it in plastic wrap and refrigerate for 2 hours.

2   TO BAKE THE DOUGH: Preheat the oven to 375°F. Butter a 9-inch pie plate. Between 2 sheets of plastic wrap, roll out the dough into an 11-inch circle, ¼ inch thick. Transfer the dough to the pie plate. Prick the bottom of the dough with a fork. Take a long piece of aluminum foil and fold it into a circle, the circumference of the pie plate. Wedge the circle over the dough onto the inside of the pie plate, gently pressing against the outer edge to hold the sides of the dough up while it bakes. Bake for 10 minutes. Remove the foil, prick the bottom again, and bake for 15 minutes more, or until the shell is baked through. Remove and cool thoroughly.

3   TO MAKE THE FILLING: Preheat the oven to 400°F. In a small saucepan, combine the heavy cream and butter and bring to a boil over low heat. Pour the cream and butter over the chocolate and whisk until combined; cool slightly. Add the egg yolks and coffee to the chocolate and stir with a wooden spoon until thoroughly mixed. Whip the egg whites with the sugar until they form stiff peaks and fold this into the chocolate mixture. Spoon the mixture into the prebaked pie shell and bake for 20 to 25 minutes, or until the filling has risen and the top feels firm to the touch.

4   TO MAKE THE SAUCE: In a heavy saucepan, bring the sugar and water to a boil and cook until golden brown and caramelized, about 10 to 20 minutes. Turn off the heat. Pour in the heavy cream, slowly because it spatters quite a bit. When the spattering stops, the caramel will have hardened on the bottom, but

(continued)

For the Chocolate Shortbread Dough:

½ cup (1 stick) unsalted butter, at room temperature
½ cup confectioners' sugar
2 tablespoons unsweetened cocoa powder
1 egg plus 1 egg yolk
1½ cups all-purpose flour
⅛ teaspoon baking soda
Pinch salt

For the Chocolate Filling:

3 tablespoons heavy cream
3 tablespoons unsalted butter
5 ounces semi-sweet chocolate bits, melted and cooled
3 eggs, separated
2 teaspoons instant espresso coffee dissolved in 1 tablespoon water
2 tablespoons granulated sugar

For the Caramel Sauce:

1 cup granulated sugar
1 cup water
¾ cup heavy cream
10 tablespoons unsalted butter
Pecan or vanilla ice cream or whipped cream (optional)

don't worry. Return the saucepan to the heat and slowly bring the mixture back to a simmer, stirring continuously to blend the caramel and cream. When the mixture feels smooth and looks well combined, remove it from the heat and cool slightly. Whisk in the butter, a tablespoon at a time, and transfer the sauce to another container. If you make this in advance, it will harden, but you may soften it by heating it for a minute in a microwave oven.

5   TO SERVE: Serve a slice of the tart surrounded by the caramel sauce and topped with a scoop of ice cream or a spoonful of whipped cream, if desired.

Four Seasons Hotel, Chicago, Illinois

Killer Fudge Cake

1 TO MAKE THE CAKE: In the top of a double boiler, over hot water, melt the butter with the unsweetened chocolate. When this is melted, remove it from the heat and transfer the mixture to a mixing bowl to cool to room temperature. While the chocolate and butter are cooling, lightly butter the bottoms of two 9-inch round cake pans and line the bottoms with parchment baking paper.

2 Preheat the oven to 350°F. When the chocolate is cool, add the eggs, sugar, salt, and vanilla and whisk together until they're well combined. Stir in the flour. Pour the batter into the prepared baking pans and bake for 35 minutes, or until a toothpick inserted in the middle comes out clean. Remove the cakes from the oven and cool them in the pans for 30 minutes. With a knife, loosen the edges of each of the cakes from the pans and turn them out onto a cake rack to cool completely.

3 TO MAKE THE ICING: While the cakes are baking, prepare the icing. In a small saucepan, combine the sugar, instant coffee, and heavy cream. Bring this to a boil, and boil gently for 6 minutes. Remove from the heat and add the unsweetened chocolate. After the chocolate has melted, add the butter and vanilla and cool to room temperature.

4 TO PUT THE CAKE TOGETHER: Set one of the cakes, top side up, on a plate and cover with a bit of icing. Set the second layer on top of the first, upside down, so the bottom is facing up, and ice the top and sides. Pat the chopped nuts onto the sides of the cake and center some in the middle of the top layer. Refrigerate the remaining icing until firm. Transfer the icing to a piping bag fitted with a rosette tip and pipe rosettes around the edges. Store the cake in the refrigerator, but bring it back to room temperature before serving.

Timbuktu, Virginia Beach, Virginia

To Make the Cake:

¾ cup (1½ sticks) unsalted butter

6 ounces unsweetened baker's chocolate

6 large eggs

3 cups sugar

½ teaspoon salt

1 tablespoon vanilla extract

1½ cups all-purpose flour

For the Icing:

1½ cups sugar

2 tablespoons instant coffee

1 cup heavy cream

5 ounces unsweetened baker's chocolate

½ cup (1 stick) unsalted butter

1 tablespoon vanilla extract

Chopped toasted pecans or walnuts for decoration

Chocolate Brownies with Ice Cream and Kahlúa

½ pound semi-sweet chocolate

1½ cups all-purpose flour

½ cup unsweetened cocoa powder

½ teaspoon baking soda

¼ teaspoon salt

1 cup (2 sticks) unsalted butter, at room temperature

2 cups sugar

5 eggs

1 teaspoon vanilla extract

2 cups chopped pecans or walnuts; or 2 cups chocolate, butterscotch, or peanut butter chips; or 1 cup chopped nuts and 1 cup chips

Ice cream of choice

Kahlúa liqueur

Baking pan tips.

(1) When you are baking in ovenproof glass, such as Pyrex, reduce the temperature by 25 degrees; clear glass transmits heat better than metal.

(2) If you're using black metal bakeware, decrease your cooking temperature by 10 degrees.

1 Preheat the oven to 350°F. Butter a 9-x-13-inch baking pan and set aside.

2 Over medium heat, melt the chocolate in the top of a double boiler over simmering water. When melted, remove from the heat and cool to room temperature.

3 In a large mixing bowl, sift together the flour, cocoa powder, baking soda, and salt and set aside.

4 In a mixer or with a wooden spoon in a separate mixing bowl, cream the butter and sugar together until light and smooth. Add the eggs, one at a time, beating well after each addition. Add the cooled melted chocolate and the vanilla.

5 Fold the sifted dry ingredients and the nuts and/or the chips into the mixture and transfer the batter to the prepared baking pan. Bake for 45 minutes; the center of the brownies will still be a little moist. Remove the pan from the oven and cool the pan on a cake rack before cutting. When cool, cut into 12 pieces.

6 TO SERVE: Center a brownie in the middle of a plate and top with ice cream. Drizzle Kahlúa liqueur on the ice cream.

Bamboleo, Las Vegas, Nevada

Devil's Food Cake

1   TO MAKE THE CAKE: Preheat the oven to 350°F. Lightly butter two 10-inch cake pans and line the bottoms with parchment paper. In a medium-sized bowl, sift together the dry ingredients. Mix the sifted ingredients with an electric hand-held mixer for 30 seconds. With the mixer still running, alternately add half the butter and 2 of the eggs, and then the remaining butter and the remaining eggs. Mix until the ingredients are evenly combined, about 1 minute. Scrape down the sides of the bowl to combine the ingredients. Continue to mix on low speed and add the buttermilk and vanilla. Increase the speed and beat the batter for 3 to 5 minutes, until it's fluffy.

2   Divide the batter between the prepared cake pans, and bake for 30 to 40 minutes, or until a cake tester or toothpick comes out clean when inserted in the center. Cool the cakes for 10 minutes, then carefully unmold them onto a cake circle or plate and cool on a rack.

3   TO MAKE THE CHOCOLATE GANACHE: Place the chocolate in a bowl. In a saucepan, bring the heavy cream to a boil. Pour the cream over the chocolate and whisk until completely smooth. Let the mixture come to room temperature and then refrigerate for 2 hours. For icing the cake, the ganache should be set but still spreadable.

4   Slice each cake horizontally into 2 layers. Set one layer on a cake circle and spread the top with about a ¼ inch of chocolate ganache. Repeat with the other layers and ganache to build the cake. Spread the top and sides of the cake with a thin, smooth layer of ganache. Chill the cake for 20 minutes.

5   Gently heat the remaining chocolate ganache in the top of a double boiler over simmering water until the ganache is pourable but not warm. To glaze the cake, set it on a rack over a pan and pour the ganache over the cake. Let the glaze drip down the sides of the cake. Chill the cake for 20 minutes. If there is extra ganache, melt it again, cool, then pour it over the cake as before.

Walt Disney World Dolphin Hotel, Orlando, Florida

For the Cake:

2¼ cups cake flour

2 cups sugar

¾ cup unsweetened cocoa powder

2 teaspoons baking powder

½ teaspoon baking soda

½ teaspoon salt

¾ cup (1½ sticks) unsalted butter, softened

4 large eggs

1¾ cups buttermilk

1 teaspoon vanilla extract

For the Chocolate Ganache:

1 pound semi-sweet chocolate, chopped into small pieces, or semi-sweet chocolate chips

2 cups heavy cream

Chocolate Surprise Cupcakes

For the Cupcakes:

1⅓ *cups all-purpose flour, sifted*

½ *teaspoon baking soda*

Pinch salt

¼ *cup unsweetened cocoa powder, sifted*

6 *tablespoons (¾ stick) unsalted butter, at
    room temperature*

1 *cup plus 2 tablespoons granulated
    sugar*

2 *eggs*

1 *teaspoon vanilla extract*

1 *cup buttermilk*

For the Filling:

½ *cup heavy whipping cream*

2 *tablespoons confectioners' sugar*

½ *teaspoon vanilla extract*

For the Icing:

4 *ounces semi-sweet chocolate, chopped*

¼ *cup water*

3 *tablespoons granulated sugar*

1 *tablespoon cold unsalted butter*

1 TO MAKE THE CUPCAKES: Preheat the oven to 350°F. Line a 12-cup muffin tin with cupcake liners. In a medium mixing bowl, resift the flour with the baking soda, salt, and cocoa powder and set aside.

2 In a large mixing bowl, cream the butter and sugar until they're light and fluffy. Add the eggs, one at a time, beating well after each addition. Add the vanilla. Then, with a wooden spoon, beat in half the buttermilk and half the flour and cocoa mixture, stirring well to combine. Add the remaining buttermilk, and remaining flour mixture and beat until thoroughly mixed. Evenly divide the batter among the muffin tins (about ¼ cup of batter per tin) and bake for 25 to 30 minutes, or until the cupcakes are springy to the touch and a toothpick inserted in the middle of a cupcake comes out clean. Cool the cupcake tin on a cake rack. When completely cool, remove the cupcakes from their paper liners.

3 TO MAKE THE FILLING: In a chilled bowl, whip the heavy cream with the sugar and vanilla until the mixture is stiff. With a small paring knife, cut out a small cone shape from the bottom of each cupcake and reserve them for later. With a knife or small spoon, remove about a teaspoonful of cake from inside each cupcake to create a hollow.

4 Fill a pastry bag fitted with a ¼-inch round tip with the whipped cream, and pipe it into the hollow (if you don't have a pastry bag, then just spoon the cream inside the cakes as best you can). Plug up the bottoms of the filled cupcakes with the reserved cake cones and set the cupcakes, bottom side down, on a baking sheet and refrigerate.

5 TO ICE THE CUPCAKES: In a small saucepan, combine the chocolate, water, and sugar and bring to a boil. When the ingredients are at a boil, lower the heat and simmer very gently, stirring on occasion, for 5 minutes exactly. Transfer the icing to a bowl, whisk in the butter, and cool until the icing has

set up a bit. Remove the cupcakes from the fridge, then pour the icing on each cupcake. With a rubber spatula, spread the icing out to the edges and refrigerate until ready to eat. Serve the cupcakes on individual plates.

Bryggen Restaurant, Trondheim, Norway

Rome's Sweet Life—Romana Sambuca

WHEN the ancient Romans first started making wine, their feel for the craft, in terms of taste, was not very good. But the good feeling that they got from drinking it kept them interested. To help the flavor along, they often mixed their wine with honey, or herbs and spices, or all of the above. One result is that the ancient Romans developed a taste for beverages that were sweet and had an herbal flavor.

Much of the time their herbal drinks were considered more in the area of medicine, than in gastronomy, but that was often the case with wines and spirits that had been given an herbal flavor. Over the centuries, one of the spirits with an herbal flavor that had a medical claim to fame and was very popular, was the *digestif,* something you drank after dinner to help you with your digestion. And one of the most popular flavors was based on anise, a flavor that many people associate with licorice.

The ancient Egyptians knew about anise, and so did the ancient Greeks. The ancient Romans often ended their banquets with anise-flavored cakes, pointing out that anise was a valuable aid to good digestion. Roman weddings usually included an anise cake for dessert.

Even today, candied almonds with an anise-flavored coating are part of weddings in France and Italy. One scholarly source tells us that at the end of an ancient Roman battle, the generals would give anise-flavored candies to their successful troops. Now, that doesn't strike me as a really great gift after a battle, but maybe there were little prizes in the boxes. The point is that for thousands of years people have associated the flavor of anise, spirits, good luck, good fortune, the end of a good battle, or the end of a good meal.

The Romans have distilled all of that into a drink called "Romana Sambuca." They drink it after dinner. They put it into espresso. Sometimes they even top off the coffee with whipped cream, ending up with a sweet anise-flavored drink they call Caffe Romana.

Roman Cheesecake

Italian ricotta cheese is less runny than what we have in America. In order to duplicate the Italian texture, we blended farmer's cheese with ricotta cheese. To help set the cake, we also added a couple of tablespoonsful of flour and an egg. I like the tang of the dried cherries, but the cake works as well with golden raisins.

1   You'll need a round cake pan, preferably with a loose bottom, 9 inches in diameter and 1½ inches deep.

2   TO MAKE THE DOUGH: In the bowl of a food processor, combine the flour, sugar, and salt, and process until blended. Add the butter and process until broken into the flour. Add the eggs and ice water to the flour and process, by pulsing several times, until the dough comes together. If the dough seems dry, add another teaspoon or so of ice water. Turn the dough onto a board and gather it into a ball. Flatten the dough slightly, wrap it in waxed paper, and refrigerate for 30 minutes.

3   Preheat the oven to 375°F.

4   Flour a pastry board and rolling pin. Remove two thirds of the dough and roll it into a circle about ¼ inch thick and 11 inches in diameter. Line the cake pan with the dough, pressing it into the bottom and up the sides of the pan. If the dough breaks apart, don't worry, just press it back into shape. Roll the remaining one third of dough into a circle about ⅜ inch thick and 10 inches in diameter. Divide this circle into 10 strips, each about ½ inch wide; this will be for the lattice top.

5   FOR THE FILLING: In a food processor, combine the ricotta and farmer's cheese, sugar, flour, egg, and Sambuca and process until smooth. Transfer the filling to a mixing bowl and fold in the pine nuts; candied orange peel; and cherries, cranberries, or golden raisins and transfer this to the dough-lined cake pan.

6   Lay 5 strips of dough across the ricotta filling and set the other 5 strips across them, at a 45° angle, to form a lattice. With a pastry brush, paint the lattice top and edges with the egg wash.

(continued)

To Make the Dough:

2½ cups all-purpose flour

¾ cup granulated sugar

¼ teaspoon salt

½ cup (1 stick) unsalted butter, at room temperature

2 large eggs, lightly beaten

1 tablespoon or more ice water

For the Filling:

One 15-ounce container whole milk ricotta cheese

One 7.5-ounce package farmer's cheese

½ cup granulated sugar

2 tablespoons flour

1 egg, lightly beaten

¼ cup Romana Sambuca liqueur

½ cup pine nuts, preferably toasted (see Note)

¼ cup finely diced candied orange peel or other dried fruit

1 cup dried cherries, cranberries, or golden raisins

Egg wash: 1 egg yolk beaten with 1 tablespoon of milk

2 tablespoons confectioners' sugar for garnish

NOTE: To toast the pine nuts, set them in a 400°F. oven for about 10 minutes. Keep an eye on them; they turn from golden to burned in seconds.

7 Set the cake pan on a baking pan and bake for 1 hour, or until the filling has set and the crust is golden. Remove the cake and cool it thoroughly on a rack before unmolding. Right before serving, shake the confectioners' sugar through a sieve to completely coat the top.

Excelsior Hotel, Rome, Italy

Pecan-Apricot Cake

Makes 8 to 10 servings

About buttermilk. Buttermilk should really be called "better milk." Contrary to what the name implies, it is actually lower in fat and calories than whole milk. Buttermilk is made with skim or low-fat milk and has less than 1 percent milk fat and only 90 to 100 calories per cup.

Originally, buttermilk was the whey left over from making butter. Before refrigeration, the buttermilk was left to clabber or thicken naturally. The modern technique blends skim milk with a buttermilk culture that causes the milk to thicken. Buttermilk is often made with salt added. If you are on a salt-restricted diet, look for buttermilk that is labeled "no salt added." In some soup recipes, buttermilk is an ideal low-calorie substitute for cream.

1   TO MAKE THE CAKE: Preheat the oven to 325°F. Lightly butter and flour a 9-inch round baking pan.

2   In a large mixing bowl, beat the eggs, honey, vegetable oil, and buttermilk together.

3   Stir in the grated carrots, whole wheat flour, baking soda, salt, and cinnamon. Add the raisins and fold in the chopped pecans.

4   Pour the batter into the prepared pan and bake for 55 minutes, or until a toothpick inserted in the center of the cake comes out dry. Remove the cake from the pan and place on a rack to cool.

5   TO MAKE THE GLAZE: In a saucepan over low heat, mix together the apricot jam, honey, and water. Stir until smooth. Brush the top of the cake with the apricot-honey glaze.

Richmond, Virginia

For the Cake:

2 eggs
½ cup honey
¾ cup vegetable oil
¼ cup low-fat buttermilk
¾ cup grated carrots
1¼ cups whole wheat flour
1 teaspoon baking soda
1 teaspoon salt
1 teaspoon ground cinnamon
¾ cup raisins
½ cup chopped pecans

For the Glaze:

1 cup apricot jam
¼ cup honey
1 tablespoon water

Pound Cake

2 cups (4 sticks) sweet unsalted butter
1 pound confectioners' sugar
6 eggs
1 pound all-purpose flour
1 teaspoon vanilla extract

About vanilla and vanilla extract. Vanilla is the pod of a climbing vine and a member of the orchid family. Vanilla extract is made from whole vanilla beans that have been soaked in alcohol. Vanillin is an artificial vanilla flavor chemically made from wood waste. By United States law, pure vanilla extract must be made from vanilla. Imitations must be labeled. When using imitation vanilla instead of pure extract, double the amount called for in the recipe.

The very best vanilla flavor comes from steeping the vanilla bean in the liquid you are using for cooking. Place a whole vanilla bean in a jar of sugar and it will give the sugar the flavor of vanilla. Long, dark brown vanilla beans can be used a number of times. Just rinse them, dry them off, and keep them in an airtight container.

1   Preheat the oven to 350°F. Butter a 9½-inch tube pan.

2   In a large bowl with an electric mixer, cream the butter and sugar together until the mixture is light and fluffy, about 5 minutes.

3   Beat in the eggs, one by one, beating well after each addition. Then add the flour to the mixture, a little at a time. Stir in the vanilla.

4   Pour into the prepared pan and bake for 1½ hours, or until a wooden toothpick inserted into the center of the cake comes out clean.

Richmond, Virginia

Coconut Cake

Makes one 2-layer 9-inch cake, serving 10 to 12

1 Preheat the oven to 350°F. Butter and flour two round 9-x-2-inch cake pans and set aside.

2 TO MAKE THE CAKE: In a mixing bowl, sift the cake flour with the baking powder. Add the salt and the coconut pudding mix and mix well with a fork or whisk to combine.

3 In a large mixing bowl, with an electric mixer, cream the shortening and sugar for 2 minutes or until they're light and airy. In alternating batches, add the sifted flour and coconut milk to the shortening-sugar mixture, beginning and ending with the flour. When the ingredients are mixed, with the electric mixer beat the batter for 30 seconds. In a clean mixing bowl, whip the egg whites with a pinch of salt until stiff and glossy. In 3 batches, fold the egg whites into the batter and transfer the batter to the prepared pans.

4 Bake for 50 to 55 minutes, or until a wooden toothpick or bamboo skewer, when inserted in the middle of the cake, comes out dry. Cool the pans on a cake rack for 20 minutes, then turn them out of the pans to cool completely.

5 TO ICE THE CAKES: With an electric mixer, whip the heavy cream with the sugar until the cream becomes stiff. Spread a ½-inch layer of the sweetened whipped cream over one layer and sprinkle 1 cup of coconut on top. Top this layer with the second layer, then spread the whipped cream on the top and sides of the cake. Pat the remaining coconut over the sides and top of the cake, making sure to press the coconut into the whipped cream so it stays anchored. Refrigerate until serving time.

Wynn's Market, Naples, Florida

For the Cake:

2¾ cups unsifted cake flour

2 teaspoons baking powder

¼ teaspoon salt

One 3.5-ounce package instant coconut pudding mix (see Note)

¾ cup vegetable shortening

1¼ cups granulated sugar

1 cup unsweetened coconut milk

5 egg whites

For the Icing:

1 quart heavy cream

½ cup confectioners' sugar

One 10-ounce package shredded sweetened coconut

NOTE: If you can't find the coconut pudding mix, then simply increase the unsifted cake flour from (2¾) cups to 3 cups and increase the granulated sugar from (1¼) cups to (1½) cups.

Orange Angel Food Cake with Orange Glaze

For the Cake:

1 cup all-purpose flour

½ cup confectioners' sugar

½ teaspoon salt

12 large egg whites, at room temperature (about 1½ cups)

1 teaspoon vanilla extract

1 teaspoon orange extract

1 tablespoon finely grated orange zest

1½ teaspoons cream of tartar

1 cup granulated sugar

For the Glaze:

1¼ cups confectioners' sugar

½ cup orange juice

1 teaspoon vanilla extract

Zest of orange, grated

1 Arrange the oven racks so the cake will sit near the bottom. Preheat the oven to 350°F.

2 TO MAKE THE CAKE: Sift the flour onto a piece of waxed paper. Measure 1 cup of the sifted flour and return it to the sifter. Discard the extra flour. Add the confectioners' sugar and salt to the flour in the sifter. Sift onto another piece of waxed paper. Sift again 4 more times and set aside.

3 In a large mixing bowl, add the egg whites, then the vanilla and orange extracts and orange zest. Beat the egg whites with the electric mixer until they are foamy. Add the cream of tartar and continue beating until they are firm, but still glossy. Add the granulated sugar, 2 tablespoons at a time. Continue beating until the egg whites cling to the sides of the bowl and are stiff but not dry. With a rubber spatula, fold in the sifted flour and confectioners' sugar mixture a little at a time. Do not stir.

4 Spoon the batter into an ungreased 10-inch tube pan. Cut through the batter with a spatula to release any large air bubbles and gently smooth the top. Bake for 45 or 50 minutes, or until cake springs back when lightly touched in the center. Cool the cake upside down on a rack for 1 hour.

5 TO MAKE THE GLAZE: In a small mixing bowl, combine the confectioners' sugar, orange juice, and vanilla. Add the grated orange zest and stir. Spoon the glaze on top of the angel cake. Spread it out to the edges with a metal spatula and let it dribble down the sides.

6 Slide a knife blade around the sides and center of the cooled cake to loosen it. Turn the cake upside down and gently lift off the pan.

7 When you're ready to serve the cake, don't cut it with a knife. Instead, insert 2 forks held back to back where you want to cut and gently tear the cake apart with the forks.

Prince Edward Island, Canada

Pear-Walnut Coffee Cake

About baking soda and baking powder. Baking soda, bicarbonate of soda, and baking powder give off carbon dioxide gas, which fizzes, creates bubbles, and helps baking mixtures rise and get lighter. Baking powder is made of a combination of ingredients and it can be used in more recipes than baking soda. Both baking soda and baking powder should be added to the liquid in the recipe quickly and at the last minute and popped right into the oven or onto the griddle.

Don't substitute baking soda for baking powder indiscriminately; some recipes call for both.

If you run out of baking powder, you can substitute as follows: 1 teaspoon baking powder = $\frac{1}{2}$ teaspoon cream of tartar, $\frac{1}{2}$ teaspoon bicarbonate of soda, and $\frac{1}{8}$ teaspoon salt.

3 cups all-purpose flour

1 teaspoon baking soda

1 teaspoon ground cinnamon

$\frac{1}{4}$ teaspoon salt

$1\frac{1}{2}$ cups (3 sticks) unsalted butter, softened

2 cups sugar

3 large eggs

2 teaspoons vanilla extract

1 cup chopped walnuts

3 cups canned pears, pieces drained (about two 16-ounce cans)

1 Heat the oven to 350°F. Lightly butter a 9-x-13-inch cake pan.

2 In a medium bowl, sift together the flour, baking soda, cinnamon, and salt. Set aside.

3 In the bowl of a standing mixer or with a hand-held mixer at low to medium speed, cream the butter and the sugar together, until the mixture is light yellow and holds soft peaks. With the mixer running, add the eggs, one at a time, fully incorporating each egg before adding the next one. Add the vanilla extract and chopped walnuts. Add the dry ingredients and mix at low speed or fold by hand, until just blended into a stiff batter. Do not overbeat the batter.

4 Fold the diced pears into the batter and spread the batter into the prepared cake pan. Smooth the top of the batter in the pan and bake for 50 minutes, or until golden brown and a cake tester or toothpick inserted in the center comes out clean. Cool the cake on a rack for 10 minutes and then unmold. Serve at room temperature.

Four Seasons Hotel, New York

Mango Strudel with Vanilla-Lime Sauce

For the Strudel:

Three 1-pound mangoes, cut into 1-inch chunks (3 cups)

2 to 3 tablespoons granulated sugar, depending upon sweetness of the fruit

6 tablespoons dry bread crumbs

½ cup finely chopped pecans

6 sheets of frozen, thawed phyllo leaves (16 × 2 inches each)

6 tablespoons melted unsalted butter

Confectioners' sugar for serving

For the Sauce:

2 cups melted vanilla ice cream

6 tablespoons fresh lime juice

1 Preheat the oven to 400°F.

2 TO MAKE THE STRUDEL: In a mixing bowl, combine the mangoes, sugar, 2 tablespoons of bread crumbs, and the pecans and and set aside.

3 Spread the phyllo leaves on a damp cloth towel, covering the top with another damp towel so the leaves do not dry out as you are working.

4 Place 1 phyllo leaf on a clean dry cloth towel and brush it with a tablespoon of melted butter using a pastry brush. Sprinkle the dough with 2 teaspoons of dry bread crumbs. Place a second leaf of phyllo on top, brush with another tablespoon of melted butter and sprinkle with 2 more teaspoons of bread crumbs. Repeat this procedure with all of the phyllo leaves.

5 Place the mango filling in a 3-inch strip along the longer edge of the dough, to within 1½ inches of the sides. Fold the sides over the filling and roll the dough into a jelly-roll shape using the cloth to help you.

6 Transfer the strudel onto a non-stick baking sheet, seam side down. Brush the top with melted butter and bake for about 25 minutes, or until the strudel is golden brown. Remove from the oven and cool for 30 minutes before serving.

7 TO MAKE THE SAUCE: Right before serving the strudel, in a bowl, blend the ice cream with the lime juice. Spoon 2 to 3 tablespoons of sauce on a plate and center a slice of strudel in the sauce. Dust some confectioners' sugar over the strudel slice and serve immediately to enjoy the contrast between the warm strudel dough and the cool sauce.

Hotel Rafael, Munich, Germany

The Gold of the Yukon

*T*HE northwest corner of Canada is known as the Yukon. It contains some of the most beautiful landscape in North America.

The people of the first nations have been living in this area for tens of thousands of years. The first Europeans to show up were the Russians. They popped in in the 1830s and began trading with the tribes on the coast. Right behind them were the English, who came in the form of the Hudson's Bay Company and began doing business with the trappers in the interior. At some point, the Hudson's Bay Company decided that they owned the territory and were therefore able to sell it to the Canadian government, which they did in 1870. The whole territory was basically ignored even by the Canadian government until 1896.

That was the year that gold was discovered, and over a million people started making plans to rush off to the Yukon. About 100,000 got started on the trip, but only about 40,000 actually made it. There had been gold rushes before—California in 1849, then in South Africa, Australia, and New Zealand, but the Klondike gold rush was the first gold rush to be treated as a media event. The Western nations were feeling the effects of a pronounced economic recession. Many people in Europe looked to North America as a land of opportunity. Many people in North America looked to the western frontier for the same reason. Combine North America, the western frontier, and tales of getting rich quick, and you have an irresistible attraction. Major newspapers around the world covered the ongoing stories every day. The reports seemed to give people a reason to hope that there was still a place in the world for the independent entrepreneur, the rugged individualist, the fortune hunter.

Most of the people rushing to the gold took a steamship from Seattle, Washington, to Skagway, Alaska, and then headed over the mountain passes into the Canadian Yukon. The passes were difficult and dangerous. Pack animals couldn't make it. And neither could most of the prospectors. The Chilkoot Trail to Lake Lindeman was only a distance of twenty miles, but much of it was on a 40-degree angle and reached up to a pass that was almost 4,000 feet high.

The White Pass was also available. It was not as steep, or as high, but it was fifteen miles longer than the Chilkoot. And if you were lucky enough to make it to the top, you would be greeted by the mounties, who were there to make sure you had a full year's worth of supplies. The average prospector had to make the climb twenty times in order to get his or her supplies to the top of the pass. And no one wanted to stop and take a rest. If you got out of line it could take hours before someone would let you get back in. Over seventy feet of snow fell on the passes that year.

Those who got through headed for the shores of Lake Lindeman or Lake Bennett and waited for the ice to break up. The area surrounding Lake Bennett was denuded of trees, which were used to build 7,000 rafts, barges, and plank ships. As soon as the spring thaw arrived, they headed off—a 500-mile ride down the Yukon River to Dawson City and the gold creeks.

The last bend in the river just before Dawson, the point where the river narrows, was a favorite fishing spot for the First Nations people. They called it *throndike,* which means "water hammer." It was the place where they hammered poles into the river bottom to trap fish. Eventually the settlers ended up pronouncing the word . . . "Klondike."

The town of Dawson is on the same slab of frozen earth where it was founded over a hundred years ago. And the turn-up into Bonanza Creek, where the gold was discovered, was the spot that was holding the world's attention.

Klondike Kate's Tin Roof Pie

Makes 6 servings

1 TO MAKE THE CRUST: In a bowl, combine the peanut butter and corn syrup with a fork, then gradually incorporate the cornflakes. When the mixture becomes hard to handle, combine the crust with your hands. Pat it down and up the sides of a 9-inch pie plate.

2 TO MAKE THE PIE: Pat the softened ice cream in the crust. Smooth the top with a rubber spatula. Wrap the pie with plastic wrap and freeze it for at least 2 hours or until the ice cream is frozen solid.

3 TO SERVE: Dip a knife into hot water and slice the pie into servings. Top with chocolate sauce, whipped cream, and chopped nuts, if desired.

Klondike Kate's, Dawson City, Canada

⅓ cup smooth peanut butter
⅓ cup dark corn syrup
2 cups crushed cornflakes
1 pint vanilla ice cream, softened
*Chocolate Sauce
    (recipe follows—optional)*
Whipped cream (optional)
*½ cup chopped pecans or walnuts
    (optional)*

Discovering gold in the Yukon

Chocolate Sauce

4 ounces semi-sweet chocolate bits

1 tablespoon sugar

12 tablespoons water

2 tablespoons Cognac, coffee, or rum

1 tablespoon unsalted butter

1 to 2 tablespoons heavy cream (optional)

1   In a small saucepan, combine the chocolate; sugar; water; and Cognac, coffee, or rum. Bring the liquid to a boil, stirring constantly, then simmer over low heat for 5 minutes, or until the sauce is slightly thickened.

2   Remove the saucepan from the heat and stir in the butter. Cool the sauce to room temperature, then refrigerate. Right before serving, stir the sauce to blend it and add the heavy cream, if desired.

Southern Pecan Pie

Makes 6 servings

1 TO MAKE THE DOUGH: In a food processor, combine the flour with the salt and sugar. Add the cold butter and shortening and pulse the machine 15 to 20 times, or until the butter and shortening have been cut into the flour in pieces about the size of oatmeal flakes. Keeping the machine running, add the water, and process, pulsing the machine on and off, for a few seconds longer or until the dough comes together. Transfer the dough to the counter and, if it is still dry, sprinkle it with a teaspoon or so of water and work the water into the dough; if the dough is too wet, dust the counter with flour and work it in. Flatten the dough into a disk, cover with plastic wrap, and chill for at least 2 hours, or preferably overnight to relax the gluten and make sure the dough isn't tough.

2 Lightly butter a 9-inch pie plate, preferably made of ovenproof glass. Lightly flour the counter and the rolling pin and roll the dough into a 10-inch circle, about ⅛ inch thick. Lift the dough into the prepared pie plate. With your thumb and index finger, pinch the edge of the dough at 1-inch intervals to create a fluted rim. Refrigerate the dough for at least 2 hours.

3 Preheat the oven to 325°F.

4 TO MAKE THE FILLING: In a mixing bowl, combine the ingredients and pour the mixture into the pie plate. Set the pie on a baking sheet and bake for 1½ hours, or until the filling is set. Cool on a wire rack.

Virginia Street Cafe, Urbanna, Virginia

For the Dough:

1 cup all-purpose flour

½ teaspoon salt

1 tablespoon sugar

2 tablespoons unsalted butter, chilled

4 tablespoons vegetable shortening, chilled

About 2 tablespoons ice water

For the Filling:

2 cups (8 ounces) pecans, coarsely chopped

4 tablespoons melted unsalted butter

¾ cup sugar

¾ cup light corn syrup

3 eggs, lightly beaten

1½ teaspoons vanilla extract

Pineapples of the Caribbean

*P*INEAPPLES have been cultivated in the Caribbean for thousands of years. Scientists reached that conclusion because the Caribbean pineapple no longer produces seeds, and that is a sign that the fruit has been farmed by man for so long that it no longer feels responsible for its own reproduction. Talk about getting lazy.

The Caribe Indians hung pineapples in front of their huts as a sign that they were home and visitors would be welcome. But they would also plant a row of pineapples at the edge of their village so that the sharp edges on the pineapple leaves would keep intruders away. Another sign with a mixed message.

Pineapples are high in vitamin C, which made them a perfect fruit for sailors who wanted to take something along to prevent scurvy. The sailors also discovered that they could plant the tops of the pineapple in the sandy soil of tropical islands, sail off, return months later, and have a fresh crop.

Caramelized Pineapple Upside-Down Tart, Harbour Island, The Bahamas

208

Caramelized Pineapple Upside-Down Tart

1 TO MAKE THE DOUGH: In a food processor, combine the flour, sugar, and salt. Add the butter and pulse the machine for 15 seconds, or until the butter is cut into the flour.

2 Add the ice water and pulse the machine until the dough just comes together; don't overprocess the dough. On a lightly floured board, pat the dough into a 6-x-½-inch disk and wrap in plastic wrap. Refrigerate for at least 2 hours.

3 TO MAKE THE TART: While the dough is resting, preheat the oven to 450°F. Lavishly butter the bottom of a 9-x-2-inch glass heatproof pie plate. Cut the pineapples in half, lengthwise, then half again, and remove the core. Cut the pineapple quarters away from the skin and cut them into ½-inch slices. Set the slices on a non-stick baking pan and roast the pineapples for 20 minutes. Drain the pineapple, then set it on paper towels to absorb any excess moisture.

4 Remove the dough from the refrigerator. Scatter half of the brown sugar on the bottom of the pie plate. Carefully set overlapping pieces of pineapple on the sugar, in a circular pattern, then top with the remaining pineapple. Scatter the remaining sugar on top. On a lightly floured board, roll the dough out into a circle about ⅛ inch thick. Set the dough on top of the pineapple and trim the dough to the edges of the pan. Tuck the edges in around the pineapple. Set the pan on a larger baking sheet to catch the drippings and bake for 1 hour. If the dough gets too brown, lightly cover it with foil.

5 Remove the tart from the oven and cool in the pan for 30 minutes. Place a platter over the tart and flip it over and out. The pineapple slices end up on top and the tart is ready to serve.

Romora Bay Club, Harbour Island, Bahamas

For the Dough:

1 cup plus 2 tablespoons all-purpose flour

2 teaspoons granulated sugar

½ teaspoon salt

5 tablespoons chilled butter, cut into ½-inch pieces

2½ to 3 tablespoons ice water

For the Tart:

Two 5-pound pineapples

3 tablespoons unsalted butter, softened, for the pan

½ cup dark brown sugar

Egg White Angel Cake

1 cup confectioners' sugar, sifted

½ teaspoon salt

1 cup cake flour, sifted

1½ cups egg whites (11 to 12 whites, depending on size)

1 teaspoon almond extract

1½ teaspoons cream of tartar

1¼ cups superfine sugar

1 Preheat the oven to 350°F.

2 In a large mixing bowl, combine the confectioners' sugar, salt, and cake flour. Then sift twice more. Set aside.

3 In a very large bowl, combine the whites, the almond extract, and cream of tartar. Beat with the electric beater or in a mixer at the highest speed, until the whites stand in peaks when you lift up the beater. Add the superfine sugar, beating only long enough after each addition to incorporate the sugar.

4 When all the sugar is in, carefully fold in the flour mixture with a spatula, a spoonful at a time, making sure all the flour is well combined, but folding only until the batter is well blended. Overmixing is fatal to angel cake.

5 Pour into an ungreased 10-inch tube pan. Bake in the center of the oven for 35 minutes, or until the cake springs back when touched lightly. Invert the pan on a funnel or over a cake rack. Allow to hang until cold. To remove the cake from the pan, run a sharp, thin-bladed knife around the side of the pan with one long steady stroke, and invert the cake on a serving plate.

Naples, Florida

Spoon Bread

1 Preheat the oven to 350°F. Lightly butter a 1½-quart casserole or 9-x-9-inch ovenproof pan.

2 In a 3-quart saucepan, whisk the cornmeal together with the milk, butter, salt, and cayenne. Slowly bring this to a boil, whisking continuously. (When it comes to a boil, it will get very thick, so whisk hard to prevent the mixture from forming lumps.) After it thickens, transfer the mixture to a mixing bowl and cool it while you separate the eggs into yolks and whites.

3 Stir the baking powder into the cornmeal mixture and mix well, then add the yolks and whisk vigorously to incorporate the yolks. In a bowl, whip the egg whites until they form stiff peaks and fold this into the cornmeal mixture.

4 Transfer the batter to the prepared pan and bake for 40 minutes, or until a wooden toothpick, when inserted into the center, comes out clean. Cut and serve portions from the pan.

Lemaire Restaurant, Jefferson Hotel, Richmond, Virginia

1½ cups yellow cornmeal

3 cups milk

½ cup (1 stick) melted unsalted butter

1 teaspoon salt

¼ teaspoon cayenne (optional)

4 eggs

½ teaspoon baking powder

Buttermilk Raisin Scones

2 cups all-purpose flour
2½ teaspoons baking powder
½ teaspoon salt
¼ cup sugar
4 tablespoons unsalted butter
1 cup raisins
1 egg
½ cup low-fat buttermilk

1   Preheat the oven to 425°F. Lightly grease a baking sheet.

2   In a large bowl, sift the flour, baking powder, and salt together. Add the sugar. Cut in the butter with a pastry blender or fork until the pieces are the size of peas. Toss in the raisins.

3   In a small bowl, combine the egg and the buttermilk.

4   Make a well in the dry ingredients and add the egg-milk mixture, stirring until combined. Do not overmix.

5   Turn the mixture onto a floured board and, with floured hands, pat the dough out into a rectangular shape about 1 inch thick. Cut the dough into 3 strips and divide each strip into 3 triangle shapes.

6   Place the scones about 2 inches apart on the baking sheet and bake for approximately 15 to 20 minutes, or until the tops are slightly golden.

The Citadel, Halifax, Nova Scotia

Peanut Butter Cookies

1 Preheat the oven to 375°F. Lightly grease 2 baking sheets.

2 In a bowl, sift the flour with the baking soda and salt.

3 In another bowl, beat the butter until it's soft. Gradually add the sugar and beat until the mixture is creamy. Add the peanut butter, egg, and vanilla to the butter-sugar mixture and mix until incorporated. Add the sifted flour mixture and mix thoroughly.

4 Roll the dough into small balls, about 1 inch in diameter, and place them on the cookie sheets. With a fork, flatten each ball, then make a mark with the tines of the fork perpendicular to the first marks so you create a cross hatch pattern.

5 Bake for 15 minutes.

Millie's Diner, Richmond, Virginia

1⅓ cups unsifted all-purpose flour
½ teaspoon baking soda
½ teaspoon salt
½ cup (1 stick) unsalted butter
1 cup sugar
1 cup natural unhomogenized peanut butter
1 large egg
½ teaspoon vanilla extract

High-Fiber Orange-Bran Muffins

1 cup whole wheat flour
½ cup all-purpose flour
1 tablespoon baking powder
¼ teaspoon baking soda
1½ cups All-Bran cereal
¾ cup skim milk
½ cup orange juice
¼ cup honey
2 egg whites
½ cup chopped dates or raisins
2 teaspoons grated orange peel

About bran. Bran is the rough outer hull of the whole wheat berry. Whole wheat flour is brown because it contains the bran of the wheat; white flour has had the bran removed.

Bran is high in B vitamins and minerals. But it is most highly prized because of its high fiber content. Bran is used as "roughage" or "bulk" because it helps keep people's digestive tracts regular. Scientists now see that a diet high in bran and dietary fiber is effective in helping to lower blood cholesterol levels and the risk of heart attack.

1   Preheat the oven to 400°F. Butter or line with paper muffin tins with 2½-inch-wide cups.

2   In a bowl, stir together the flours, baking powder and soda, and set aside.

3   In a large bowl, mix together the cereal, milk, and orange juice. Let stand for 3 minutes. Add the honey, egg whites, dates or raisins, and orange peel, and beat well.

4   Add the dry ingredients to the cereal mixture, stirring only until combined. Spoon the batter into the muffin tins, filling each cup about two-thirds full.

5   Bake for about 20 minutes, or until the muffins are golden brown. Cool on a rack.

Toronto, Canada

High-Protein, High-Fiber, Low-Fat Egg White Pancakes

Makes 13 pancakes, 4 inches in diameter

½ cup yellow cornmeal
½ cup whole wheat flour
½ cup enriched white flour
1½ cups skim milk
3 egg whites
1 cup non-fat plain yogurt

1 In a large mixing bowl, mix together the cornmeal, whole wheat flour, and white flour. Blend in the skim milk and allow the batter to stand for 5 minutes.

2 In a separate bowl, whip the egg whites until they stand in peaks. Then fold them into the batter.

3 Preheat a non-stick skillet and spoon in the batter. Cook until bubbles form on the pancake or the edges turn brown, then flip the pancake over and cook for 1 minute more.

4 Top each with a dollop of non-fat plain yogurt.

Burt Wolf's Kitchen, New York City

Blueberry Muffins

½ cup whole milk

¼ cup vegetable oil

1 egg

1 tablespoon vanilla extract

1 cup fresh blueberries, or 1 cup frozen
  blueberries, thawed and drained

1½ cups all-purpose flour

½ cup sugar

2 teaspoons baking powder

Dash salt

1 Preheat the oven to 400°F. Grease 10 muffin cups or line them with cupcake papers.

2 In a medium bowl, combine the milk, oil, egg, and vanilla. In another bowl, toss the blueberries with 2 tablespoons of the flour and set aside.

3 Add the remaining flour, sugar, baking powder, and salt to the liquid ingredients. Stir to combine. Add the blueberries and stir to combine. The batter should be lumpy; do not overmix.

4 Fill the muffin cups about two-thirds full with the batter. Bake for 20 to 25 minutes, until the muffins are golden and a wooden toothpick inserted in the center of a muffin comes out clean. Cool on a rack.

Charlevoix, Quebec

Lemon-Yogurt Muffins

Makes 12 Muffins

About zest. Zest is the grated outer peeling of lemons, oranges, limes, and grapefruits. The best way to add zest to your cooking is to rub the whole fruit against the tiny holes on a small hand grater or a zester.

The zest is more flavorful than the juice of the fruit because it has a very high oil content. Be sure to use only the colorful outer rind, because the white connective tissue right underneath is very bitter.

2 cups all-purpose flour
½ cup Cream of Wheat cereal
½ cup granulated sugar
2 teaspoons baking powder
½ teaspoon baking soda
2 large eggs
1 cup non-fat plain yogurt
6 tablespoons skim milk
2 tablespoons grated lemon zest
1 tablespoon vegetable oil
4 tablespoons dark brown sugar

1 Preheat the oven to 350°F. Coat a 12-cup muffin tin with oil.

2 Into a large bowl, sift the flour, Cream of Wheat, granulated sugar, baking powder, and baking soda; mix to combine evenly. In another bowl, whisk together the eggs, yogurt, milk, and lemon zest. Add the wet ingredients to the dry ingredients and stir with a wooden spoon until just blended.

3 Spoon the batter into the muffin cups, filling each one two thirds of the way up. Sprinkle the top of each with 1 teaspoon of the brown sugar.

4 Bake the muffins for 20 minutes, or until a cake tester or tooth-pick comes out clean when inserted into the center of a muffin. Cool in the pan for 5 minutes, then turn the muffins out onto a wire rack to cool completely.

Four Seasons Hotel, New York

Triple Berry Muffins

Vegetable oil spray

3 large eggs

*¼ cup brown sugar, packed,
    plus 2 tablespoons for tops*

½ cup vegetable oil

½ cup whole milk

2 tablespoons bran

1 teaspoon baking powder

1 teaspoon baking soda

½ teaspoon salt

1 cup whole wheat flour

1 cup unbleached all-purpose flour

*¾ cup raspberries, cranberries,
    or blueberries; or ¼ cup each
    of each type of berry*

About raspberries. Raspberries grow better in countries in northern latitudes. Most raspberries are red, but they can also be black, yellow, golden, or white. Raspberries are a good source of vitamin C. They have naturally high amounts of pectin, which makes them perfect for jams and jellies.

1   Preheat the oven to 375°F. Line a 12-cup muffin tray with paper liners or spray them with a non-stick vegetable oil spray.

2   In a large mixing bowl, with a whisk, blend the eggs with the ¼ cup of brown sugar, and whisk until frothy. Add the oil and milk and beat until blended. Blend in the bran.

3   In a separate mixing bowl, with a whisk or fork, combine the dry ingredients. Gradually incorporate the dry ingredients into the egg mixture and beat with a wooden spoon until the batter is smooth. Fold in the berries and let the batter set for 5 minutes.

4   Fill the muffin tins three quarters full and sprinkle about ½ teaspoon of brown sugar over each muffin. Bake for 22 to 25 minutes, or until a toothpick inserted in the center of the muffin comes out dry. Cool on a rack. Store in the refrigerator.

The Chocolate Claim, Whitehorse, Canada

Fruit Tartlets

Makes six 3½-inch tarts

1 TO MAKE THE DOUGH: In a food processor, combine the flour with the salt. Add the butter and shortening and pulse 15 to 20 times, or until the butter and shortening are about the size of oatmeal flakes. While the machine is running, add the ice water and process, pulsing the machine on and off, for a few seconds longer, or until the dough comes together. Transfer the dough to the counter and, if it is still dry, sprinkle it with a teaspoon or so of water and work the water into the dough. Flatten the dough into a disk, wrap in plastic wrap, and chill, preferably overnight, or for at least 2 hours.

2 TO ROLL OUT THE DOUGH: Lightly flour the counter. Divide the dough into 6 even pieces. Roll out each piece of dough into a circle, about 4 inches in diameter. Drop the dough into fluted 3½-inch tartlet shells, and press it in. Prick the bottom surface with the tines of the fork. Repeat this procedure with all of the tartlet shells and refrigerate them for an hour.

3 TO PREBAKE THE TARTLET SHELLS: Preheat the oven to 375°F. Line the tartlet shells with pieces of foil and then put in pie weights or beans or lentils, filling each tartlet shell to the top. Bake for 10 minutes. Remove the tartlet shells and cool for a minute, then remove the weights and the foil. If the bottom of the dough begins to lift up, prick it with a fork. Return the shells to the oven to bake completely for another 15 minutes, or until golden brown. Remove and cool completely.

4 TO FINISH THE TARTLETS: In a small saucepan, warm the jam. With a pastry brush, paint the inside of the prebaked tartlet shells with the jam and cool completely. Spread some whipped cream over the jam. Attractively arrange an assortment of mango and kiwi slices, raspberries or blueberries, and straw-berry slices over the whipped cream and chill the tartlet shells until serving time. Right before serving, dust the fruit lightly with confectioners' sugar.

Naples Beach Hotel and Golf Club, Naples, Florida

For the Dough:

1½ cups all-purpose flour

Pinch salt

½ cup butter (1 stick), cut into tablespoon-sized pieces

4 tablespoons shortening, chilled

4 to 5 tablespoons ice water

For the Tart:

½ cup apricot jam or raspberry jam, strained

About 2 cups lightly sweetened whipped cream

1 mango, pitted and cut into very thin slices

1 kiwi, peeled and cut into very thin slices

1 cup fresh raspberries or blueberries

6 strawberries, trimmed and each one cut into thin slices

Confectioners' sugar

Fruit Tartlet, The Naples Beach Hotel and Golf Club, Naples, Florida

Figgy Duff

1½ cups dried bread crumbs

⅓ cup all-purpose flour

¾ cup raisins, soaked in 3 tablespoons of rum until plump, drained

¼ teaspoon ground allspice

¼ teaspoon ground cinnamon

¼ teaspoon grated nutmeg

½ teaspoon baking powder

½ cup dark molasses or dark corn syrup

5 tablespoons melted butter

3 tablespoons dark rum

3 quarts water

Maple syrup to taste

1 cup whipped cream

12 strawberries, sliced

About strawberries. An Englishman once said of the strawberry, "Doubtless the Almighty could make a better berry—but He never did." Strawberries grow wild on many continents. They were so abundant in New England that an early colonist said you couldn't put your foot down without stepping on one.

Strawberries were always the first fruit of spring in temperate zones. The strawberry season used to last from 1 to 3 months, but with new breeds and methods, it now runs from February through November in California. Production is greatest in May.

When buying strawberries, look for clean, bright berries with a uniform red color. Their green stem caps should be attached. Don't wash or remove the stems until right before you eat them. Strawberries should be used the day of purchase.

1 In a large mixing bowl, combine the bread crumbs, flour, soaked raisins, spices, baking powder, molasses, butter, and rum.

2 Transfer the mixture to a plastic bag (but don't close it) and wrap the bag in a double thickness of cotton cheesecloth. Tie the bag securely at the top.

3 In a large pot, bring the water to a boil and add the wrapped pudding. Cover and simmer over low heat for 1½ hours. Remove the pudding from the water and drain. When cool enough to handle, unwrap the pudding and transfer it to a cutting board.

4 Slice the pudding into 6 wedges. Spoon maple syrup on each serving plate and place a wedge of pudding on the syrup. Spoon a dollop of whipped cream next to the pudding and garnish the whipped cream with sliced strawberries.

Hotel Newfoundland, Newfoundland, Canada

DESSERTS AND CANDIES

Chocolate Mousse

Honey Flan

Four Berry Dessert

Raspberries in Raspberry Sauce

Peach Cobbler

Tiramisù

Zabaglione

The Dandoy Cookies of Brussels

DANDOY is one of the most famous cookie shops in the world. It was opened by the Dandoy family in 1829, in the Belgian city of Brussels.

Dandoy's most famous cookie is a type of gingerbread called *speculoos,* which are traditionally given to good children on St. Nicholas Day, the sixth of December. The word *speculoos* is Latin and it means "mirror." The cookies come out of hand-carved wooden forms that mirror the image of St. Nicholas.

Dandoy also makes a series of cookies in the shape of animals. The idea of baking something in the form of an animal goes back for thousands of years.

When a well-to-do person in ancient Greece needed a little help from the gods, he would offer an animal along with his request. But not so well-to-do people couldn't afford to give up their animal, so they offered some dough in the form of an animal. And that is how animal cookies got their start.

Over the centuries, these pictorial cookies were used to mark an event or tell a story and their shapes became more and more elaborate.

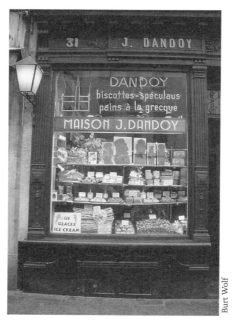

Dandoy Cookie Shop, Brussels, Belgium

Chocolate Mousse

About chocolate and health. Chocolate is perfectly acceptable as part of a balanced diet. A 1-ounce milk chocolate bar contains 147 calories. Furthermore, studies have shown that bacteria in the skin, not chocolate, is the cause of acne in teenagers. Eating chocolate does not increase your chances of getting cavities any more than any other food.

A 1.5-ounce milk chocolate bar contains 9 milligrams of caffeine. That is only one tenth of the amount in a cup of coffee. Researchers have also disproven the idea that chocolate inhibits the body's ability to use calcium and that chocolate causes hyperactivity in children.

6 ounces semi- or bittersweet chocolate, finely chopped

1 ounce unsweetened chocolate, finely chopped

½ cup low-fat milk

1 tablespoon Grand Marnier or dark rum, or 1 teaspoon vanilla extract (optional)

1 cup heavy cream

¼ cup confectioners' sugar, sifted

Sweetened whipped cream for garnish (optional)

1   In a small, heavy saucepan over very low heat, melt the semi-sweet and unsweetened chocolates along with the milk, stirring continuously. When melted, transfer the mixture to a clean bowl, and add the Grand Marnier or vanilla if you wish. Let this mixture stand until cool to the touch yet still fluid. (If you don't cool it long enough, the chocolate will seize into tiny flecks as you fold it into the whipped cream.)

2   When the chocolate is cool, whip the cream with an electric beater or in a stationary mixer until it stands in soft peaks. Add the confectioners' sugar and beat until the mixture is stiff. (Take care not to overwhip or you'll end up with butter.)

3   Add some of the chocolate to the whipped cream and fold together, using a whisk. Add the remaining chocolate and fold until just combined. Transfer the mousse to 6 wine goblets or ramekins, and refrigerate until serving time. (Serve within a day of making.)

4   If you wish, right before serving, transfer some whipped cream to a pastry bag fitted with a star tip and pipe a rosette of whipped cream in the center of each mousse.

Hotel Metropole, Brussels, Belgium

Honey Flan

½ cup orange blossom honey to caramelize the ramekins, plus 3 tablespoons and 2 teaspoons (see Note)

3 eggs

1½ cups half and half or light cream

2 teaspoons vanilla extract

1 Granny Smith apple

2 Red Delicious apples

1 tablespoon fresh lemon juice

1 pint strawberries

3 tablespoons unsalted butter

18 whole blackberries

6 sprigs fresh mint for garnish

About honey. Honey is the nectar of flowers collected and pressed by bees. We get the sticky fluid by spinning the combs of the hives and extracting the honey.

Honey develops different flavors depending on the type of flower from which the bees get their nectar. Clover is by far the most common, but there is also dark rich buckwheat honey, fragrant lavender honey, tupelo honey, and orange-blossom honey.

From a sugar-calorie standpoint, there is no difference between table sugar and honey. Honey just has a different taste. When using honey in cooking, a straight cup-for-cup substitution is acceptable, but honey will change the flavor, color, and liquidity of the dish.

It is best to store honey in a closed container at room temperature. If it crystallizes and hardens, place it in warm water until it liquefies.

1 TO PREPARE THE RAMEKINS: Heat a medium sauté pan over high heat, or until very hot. Add the ½ cup of honey and cook over medium heat until the honey is a dark brown. Pour the honey into six ½-cup porcelain or ovenproof ramekins. With a potholder to protect your hands, tilt each ramekin so the honey coats the bottom and sides. Preheat the oven to 350°F.

2 TO MAKE THE FLAN: In a mixing bowl combine the eggs, half and half, 3 tablespoons of honey, and vanilla. Ladle this custard mixture into the prepared ramekins and set the ramekins in a baking pan filled with enough hot water to reach halfway up the outside of the ramekins. Bake for an hour, or until the flans are set and no longer wobbly.

3 TO MAKE THE FRUIT GARNISH: While the flans are baking, core, peel, and cut the apples into ¼-inch dice. Toss them with some lemon juice so they do not discolor. Stem the strawberries and cut them into quarters.

NOTE: Orange blossom honey gives this recipe a special flavor, but you can use any honey you like.

4   TO FINISH THE FLAN AND GARNISH: Remove the baking pan
    from the oven and remove the ramekins from the baking pan.
    In a 10-inch skillet over high heat, heat the butter. When the
    butter turns golden brown, add the apples and sauté over high
    heat for about a minute, or until the apples take on some
    color. Add the remaining 2 teaspoons of honey and remove the
    skillet from the heat. Toss in the strawberries and stir to com-
    bine.

5   With a knife, loosen the edges of the custards from the
    ramekins and turn each one, upside down, in the middle of a
    dessert plate. Not all the caramelized honey will come out.
    Spoon the apples and strawberries around the flan and set 3
    blackberries over the fruit. Garnish each flan with a sprig of
    mint.

La Mansion del Rio, San Antonio, Texas

Four Berry Dessert

½ pint blackberries

½ pint blueberries

½ pint raspberries

1 pint strawberries

One 10-ounce package frozen raspberries in light syrup, thawed

Selection of 2 or more fruit sorbets of choice

Mint leaves for garnish

About mint. Spearmint and peppermint are the two most common and useful culinary mints; there is very little difference in their flavors. Both are native to Europe but they are fully naturalized in America. Gracious homes of the Old South always grew a mint bed for adding to Bourbon whiskey.

Mint is a cooling and refreshing herb. In Arab countries, it is common to see people walking home from the market with large bunches of fresh mint stalks in their hands. It is made into mint tea, very strong and heavily sweetened. Roast lamb with mint jelly is a traditional English and American favorite.

1 Prepare the fruits by picking through the berries, discarding any which are bruised or moldy. Stem the strawberries and, if large, cut them in half.

2 Puree the frozen raspberries in a blender or food processor until they're smooth, and strain through a sieve.

3 In each of 6 glass goblets or shallow bowls, portion out 1 cup of mixed berries and 2 small scoops of sorbet; drizzle about ⅓ cup of sauce over the berries and garnish with mint.

The Ritz-Carlton, Naples, Florida

Raspberries in Raspberry Sauce

1 If you are using frozen raspberries, thaw them in the refrigerator just until the berries are separated but still icy. Don't do this too far ahead of time. The berries should still have a few ice crystals in their hearts at serving time.

2 In an electric blender, puree about one quarter of the berries, adding superfine sugar to taste. How much sugar to use will depend on the character of the fruit and the taste of the cook; taste as you go.

3 If you want a seedless sauce, press the puree through a fine sieve. Add a little Kirsch or framboise liqueur, if desired.

4 Spoon fresh raspberries into serving dishes and top with the puree.

Munich, Germany

3 pints fresh or frozen raspberries, plus extra for serving
Superfine sugar
Kirsch or framboise liqueur (optional)

Peach Cobbler

8 ripe peaches; or 6 cups sliced frozen
   peaches, thawed

1 tablespoon honey

1 tablespoon sugar

Grated zest of 1 orange (optional)

¼ teaspoon ground cinnamon

Pastry for two 9-inch crusts, rolled to
   ¼-inch thickness

2 tablespoons whole milk

Low-fat frozen yogurt or ice cream for
   serving

1 Preheat the oven to 350°F.

2 If using fresh peaches, in a large stockpot bring 4 quarts of water to a boil. Drop the peaches in the boiling water for 30 seconds. Refresh in cold water. Peel the peaches and remove the pits.

3 Chop the peaches and place in a large mixing bowl. Stir in the honey, sugar, orange zest (if used), and cinnamon. Divide the mixture evenly into eight 6-ounce custard dishes.

4 Cut the pastry into 8 rounds, slightly larger than the custard dishes. Lay the pastry over the dishes and let the excess hang over the sides. Crimp lightly with a fork around the rim. Make several slits to allow the steam to escape. Brush the crust with the milk. Place on a baking sheet and bake for 30 to 35 minutes.

5 Serve warm with low-fat frozen yogurt or ice cream.

The Sea Grill, New York City

The Sweet Life of Italy

*I*TALY is famous for its sweet confections and pastries, and there are historical reasons for this notoriety. For thousands of years, honey was the primary sweetening in the human diet. And during those years, it became a symbol for goodness and purity. For centuries, honey lived its sweet life without competition. And then, in the eleventh century, things began to change. Sugar arrived from the East, and Western food has never been the same.

We know that for at least 2,000 years sugar has been in use in both the near and Far East. We know that the Arabs brought sugar to Sicily and Spain during the 700s. We also know that no one in Europe paid much attention to sugar until the time of the Crusades. The Crusaders got a really good look at the stuff in Tripoli and very soon thereafter it was being imported to Europe by the traders in Venice. But for over four hundred years, it was rare, it was expensive, it was used only as a spice or a medicine, and only by the very rich.

Nevertheless, from the very beginning of its use in Europe, we can document an increase in the number of recipes using sugar. Our sweet tooth had begun to grow, and when sugar production got started in the Caribbean, the sugar business took off. Suddenly there was a clear increase in the use of sugar in place of honey. As sugar became more and more available, and at a lower and lower price, the general public began to use it as much as possible.

Sugar made average people feel that they were eating like a king. And sugar became an important item of international trade, which was never the case with honey. Sugar was big business, and it was a sweet deal for the governments that taxed it. Sugar became the first luxury to end up as a mainstay in the diet of an entire continent.

But even in the early years when sugar was coming into Europe as a rare and expensive spice, the Italians were developing pastry and candy recipes that used sugar as the sweetening agent. The Italians also began to develop an international reputation for their skill with sugar. They were so well thought of in this area, that up until the last century it was the custom for wealthy households to employ Italian pastry cooks and confectioners along with their French chefs.

Panettone

*M*ANY of the early European specialists in pastry and confectionery were from northern Italy. Northern Italians had learned about sugar from the Arabs who were living in Sicily and from the Crusaders who brought it back to Europe in the 1100s. Northern Italians also had easy access to the spices that were coming in through Venice. One of the earliest recorded examples of their skills deals with a recipe for a cake called "Panettone." There are lots of stories about how Panettone got started, but the most popular is set in Milan during the year 1490.

Once upon a time, there was a young nobleman who fell in love with the daughter of a baker named Toni. To impress the girl's father, the young man disguised himself as a baker's assistant and went to work in Toni's bake shop. While he was there, he invented a sweet, delicate, dome-shaped yeast bread made of flour, eggs, milk, butter, raisins, and candied fruit. The cake became wildly popular and people came to the bakery from far and wide to buy what was called *Pan de Toni,* which translates into English as "Toni's bread." The young man became a hero to the father, the marriage of the young nobleman and Toni's daughter was a glorious event, and everyone lived happily ever after—with the possible exception of the nobleman's lawyers, who never realized that Panettone would become popular throughout the world and therefore failed to trademark the name or the recipe.

Pandoro

 $\mathcal{P}$ ANDORO, which means the "bread of gold," originated in the city of Verona, the home of Romeo and Juliet. Some historians believe that in the 1400s, when the Venetian Republic was using recipes to display their wealth and power, Pandoro got started as a cake that was covered in gold leaf. During the 1700s, when Venice was not doing as well, Pandoro evolved into a Christmas cake in the shape of a tree with a powdered sugar star on top. It's a rich cake made with eggs, butter, and sugar. Today, it's no longer confined to the Christmas season and often comes to the table as a dessert stuffed with ice cream, topped with fruit, or drizzled with a rum sauce.

Panforte

 $\mathcal{T}$ HE story of panforte begins in a nunnery in Siena. In order to take a census of the local population, the head of the nunnery asked everybody in the neighborhood to bring in a cake made from spices and honey. The nuns liked the result, made it an annual event, and eventually the recipe became standardized into what we now call "panforte." The most popular version is called "Margherita" and was first produced in 1879 to mark a state visit of Queen Margherita of Savoy to the town of Siena. I'll bet you didn't know any of that. And I hope it improves your appreciation of panforte.

Torrone

*J*UST about everything on the Italian menu comes with a story. One of the most unusual is the tale of torrone. On October 24, 1441, Bianca Maria Visconti married Francesco Sforza. These two came from the most important families in Milan and the wedding was a major social event. The bride's dowry contained an extraordinary collection of things—including the city of Cremona just outside of Milan. I love that. "Marry my daughter and I will give you this nice little city as a wedding gift." The mind boggles. So Sforza gets Cremona, and the bakers of the city commemorate the event by making a candy in the shape of the tower. Actually, the tower's considerably bigger than this, this is just a scale model. It's made from almonds and honey and whipped egg whites that have been baked for hours.

Big hit at the wedding. And the guests who had come from all over Europe began asking for samples of the torrone to take back home. These days, the tower is somewhat modified in form, looks more like the Twin Towers of the World Trade Center in New York City, but the confection is more popular than ever.

The Colomba

*T*HE Colomba is a yeast cake made with butter, egg yolks, milk, sugar, orange peel, and almonds. It has a soft and delicate texture, a golden crust, it always comes in the shape of a dove, and has been associated with Easter for many centuries. It is a traditional dessert at Easter time.

The Colomba is said to have originated as a result of the Battle of Legnano, which took place just after Easter in 1176. Things were not going well for the Milanese as they defended their city against an attack by Barbarossa . . . until three doves flew out of a nearby church. The birds appear to have flown an air-support mission that dropped bad luck on Barbarossa and delivered victory to the Milanese. The cake reminds Milan of this triumph.

Baci

*B*ACI is the Italian word for "kisses," and it has been applied to this candy since 1907. Young Giovanni Buitoni had been sent by his family to set up a candy factory in Perugia. Luisa Spagnoli was the product developer. They fell in love but were forced to keep their relationship a secret. They exchanged their messages of love by wrapping notes in the chocolate samples that they sent up and back between them. Today, Baci contains a message of love in every package to commemorate that relationship.

Italian Biscotti

THE baking of biscotti in Italy became important during the 1600s when the Venetian navy began searching for foods that would not go bad at sea. They realized that dried cookies would be perfect, and set up a Biscotti Procurement Office. I would have liked to have worked there. During the 1800s, the manufacturers widened their audience, in more ways than one, by marketing their biscotti to the upper classes. They designed all of their packaging to attract the rich and famous. *Biscotti,* by the way, is not the Italian word for "biscuit"; it means "twice baked."

Milan

MILAN has been an important city for well over 2,000 years. It was a significant political and commercial center for the Roman Empire, and it has maintained that position ever since. The name *Milan* comes from an ancient word meaning "the center of the plain." It's a reference to the fact that Milan was built in the middle of the Po Valley plain, a crossing point for a number of roads that came down out of the Alps and connected to the commercial trade routes in what is now Italy.

Milan, Italy

Tiramisù

In Italy, the filling for a traditional tiramisù is made by blending mascarpone cheese with raw egg yolks and then lightening the mix by blending it with whipped egg whites. Because raw eggs carry the risk of salmonella, in our filling, we have omitted them entirely and added a bit more whipped cream for volume and lightness

1 cup water

6 tablespoons sugar

2 tablespoons "instant" espresso coffee

¼ cup sweet Marsala wine
    or orange juice

1 cup (8 ounces) mascarpone cheese
    or other mild cream cheese

1 teaspoon vanilla extract

¼ cup dark rum, Cognac, or orange juice

1 cup heavy cream

8 ounces lady fingers, Italian "Savoiardi"
    cookies, sponge cake,
    or angel food cake cut into pieces
    about ½ inch thick, 2 inches long,
    and 1 inch wide

1 tablespoon unsweetened cocoa powder
    for garnish

1   TO MAKE THE ESPRESSO SOAKING SYRUP: Set aside a 13-×-9-inch glass baking pan. In a small saucepan, bring the water, 3 tablespoons of the sugar, and the instant espresso coffee to a boil. Remove the saucepan from the heat and cool to room temperature. When cool, add the Marsala wine and transfer the mixture to a shallow plate.

2   TO MAKE THE FILLING: In a bowl, blend the mascarpone together with the remaining 3 tablespoons of sugar, vanilla, and rum and 2 tablespoons of the espresso soaking syrup. Beat until smooth. Whip the cream until it's stiff and fold it into the cheese mixture.

3   TO ASSEMBLE THE TIRAMISÙ *(see Note):* Quickly dip the lady fingers or cake pieces (don't saturate them) on both sides into the espresso syrup and make one layer of dipped cake in the baking pan. Top with half of the mascarpone and whipped cream mix. Dip the remaining cookies in the espresso syrup and create a second layer. Evenly spread the remaining half of the mascarpone and whipped cream mix over the top. Cover the baking pan with plastic wrap and refrigerate for at least 2 hours. The Tiramisù can be prepared a day or two ahead. Right before serving, dust the top of the Tiramisù with unsweetened cocoa powder. Serve cold.

Hotel Principe di Savoia, Milan, Italy

NOTE: To make individual servings of Tiramisù, first create some steel ring molds by removing the tops and bottoms of tuna fish cans and washing the remaining rings well. Set the rings on individual plates and line each one with some soaked sponge cake, then a layer of mascarpone, a layer of soaked sponge cake, and a layer of mascarpone. Cover and refrigerate for at least 2 hours. Right before serving, carefully remove the steel ring and dust the top with unsweetened cocoa powder.

Milan's Hotel Principe di Savoia

MILAN'S Hotel Principe di Savoia opened in 1927 and was designed as a new type of hotel. There had been luxury hotels for tourists, and there had been efficient hotels for business travelers, but the Principe was the first hotel designed to meet the needs of the traveling business executive in surroundings that were luxurious.

Today, the Principe di Savoia is part of ITT Sheraton's Luxury Collection, and the original objectives are still being pursued. The main bar looks like the winter gardens that were popular at the turn of the century—a courtyard enclosed by a dome of glass. The Cafe Doney serves pastries and an afternoon tea the way it did decades ago.

Zabaglione, Hotel Principe di Savoia, Milan, Italy

Zabaglione

5 large egg yolks

5 tablespoons sugar

12 tablespoons sweet Marsala wine

Lady fingers or Savoiardi cookies
   for serving

1   Set up a double boiler or a medium-size stainless-steel bowl over a pot of simmering water. Check to make sure the bottom of the bowl is not touching the water, or the eggs may scramble.

2   With a hand-held electric mixer, beat the egg yolks and sugar together until pale yellow. Add the Marsala and set the bowl over the simmering water. Continue to beat with the electric mixer until the eggs triple in volume, thicken, and reach a temperature of 140°F., as registered on an instant thermometer. Be sure to beat the eggs until they reach this temperature at which salmonella bacteria is killed. This will take about 10 to 15 minutes. Be sure to move the beater around the bowl so the eggs cook evenly; there will be quite a bit of spattering.

3   Transfer the mixture to wineglasses and serve immediately accompanied by lady fingers or Italian cookies known as Savoiardi.

4   An alternative way to serve this is to take slices of pound cake or panettone and set them on a broiler pan. Cover the cake slices with a layer of sliced strawberries or peeled Comice pear, and ladle a portion of the zabaglione over the fruit. Broil the slices for a minute, or until the zabaglione is bubbling and lightly browned. Serve immediately.

Hotel Principe di Savoia, Milan, Italy

INDEX